How Relationships Work

John K. Pollard, III

Published by

Generic Human Studies Publishing

9815 N. 95th Street, Scottsdale, AZ 85258 USA

Phone: 925-858-3137

Library of Congress Cataloging-in-Publication Data CIP Data Pending Publication Date Oct 2008

ISBN 0942055292

Dedication:

This book is dedicated to Dennis Gottlieb,
the one person I know
who most fulfilled its promise.

Contents

Preface

The basic premise for How Relationships Work came to me in February 1986. By this time I'd exhausted the range of new age religions and self-help seminars that I had begun studying twenty years earlier. I was publishing my first book, *SELF-PARENTING: The Complete Guide To Your Inner Conversations*, an innovative self-help system that was the culmination of 10 years of extensive study and personal research. Because of all the "inner" work I'd been doing, I truly felt my personal "inner" life was successful and going smoothly.

I must say, however, on the level of what I had begun to call my "outer" relationships, I still was not satisfied. In fact, in certain situations I was decidedly unhappy. Many of my relationships just didn't feel like they were going the way they should. I was also struggling with that classic new age cliché everyone seemed to believe:

"Once you are right on the inside, all your relationships will be right on the outside."

This was becoming a problem for me; my relationships were not "right." But if anybody was "right on the inside," it was me. Since 1968 I had studied and practiced advanced body, mind, and spiritual disciplines with the outstanding teachers in these areas. In the mid '70s I became a Chiropractor, and after graduation I worked hard to develop one of L.A.'s first genuine multidisciplinary healing clinics. Because I lived frugally and conserved my savings, I earned financial independence, retiring stress-free on the beach in Malibu at the age of 38. And yet, with all this measure of personal success, I still wasn't satisfied. It seemed to me that too high a percentage of my outer relationships were simply not supporting me positively.

Try to understand this from a certain perspective. I was happy being involved in the relationships, but not with the relationships themselves. For example, even though I was "right on the inside," my neighbor was being horrendous to me. Also, one of my team members in the clinic, whom I felt I'd helped a great deal, was stealing money from the till. And a big one was my father. Despite having finally achieved social status in society's terms (such as being a doctor, having financial independence, etc.), he was still being his typical "negative self," so nothing I did was good enough to earn his love.

Here I was, happy on the inside through positive Self-Parenting and happy in society's eyes through hard work and achievement. Yet a large proportion of my relationships with other people were unfulfilling, particularly as I was giving them my best effort and using all my success skills to try to "make them work."

Why were my personal relationships so unfulfilling, so hit-and-miss, so up and down? What was missing? Was it me? Was it Los Angeles? Why were so many relationship problems continuing to happen to me?

Plus, the harder I tried, the worse things turned out—if not immediately, then eventually later. So I started questioning this new age commandment, this unassailable truth about "being right on the inside," because it wasn't working for me. I needed some new answers.

What you will find in this book are the results of that mission and the subsequent twenty years of research and development that culminated in these findings. I immersed myself completely in researching academic, sociological, and psychological theories on relationships. To be fair, any new material I learned also had to be consistent with my already rather extensive accumulated knowledge in personal development.

For example, one principle of consciousness growth states, "anything that goes wrong in a relationship is your perception and evaluation alone." If you are upset about something in a relationship, you are supposed to work on your own consciousness until you no longer experience the "addictive demand" that's making you unhappy. Although I believed this quite strongly, I also intuitively felt there had to be some new factors to be discovered that might explain my relationship problems. I was doing the above but it wasn't helping.

The big breakthrough, the proverbial apple falling on Newton's head, came one summer evening at Cremorne Point, in Sydney, Australia. After a full day of writing and editing on the computer, I decided to relax by going for a stroll along Sydney Harbor. For weeks I had been struggling, trying to find a key that would unite all the material with which I was working. Cremorne Point is a beautiful natural outcrop on the incredible Sydney Harbor, directly across from the sparkling Opera House. I was by myself, breathing, relaxing, and enjoying the night air. It was long after midnight.

Walking by the children's play area, I impulsively jumped up on the middle of a seesaw (teeter-totter) and stood there, balancing and rocking on my feet. At that moment, the key to my dilemma popped into my entire being. I realized that if I really wanted to make this seesaw work properly, I couldn't stand in the middle all the time, trying to keep both sides balanced. What I really wanted and intuitively knew to be correct was that I was supposed to get on only one side of the seesaw. So that's what I did.

As I sat there still not feeling fulfilled, I noticed the higher side and thought to myself, "What I really want is to be up there." So I moved over to the high side and sat down. You can guess what happened next. Waiting there, essentially alone, for someone to get on the other side of the seesaw, I intuitively understood my problem.

In those few seconds I finally understood that a relationship functions exactly the same way a seesaw is structured. A relationship requires two people to be on the same seesaw; one at either end (not on the same side, in the middle, or on a different seesaw), and that's when the whole system clicked into place.

My problems with personal relationships suddenly became almost all too clear. With my new understanding, I spent the next four months writing, evaluating, and discussing these "seesaw" concepts with others. These principles became a major part of the philosophy I created and developed during that time, which I called Generic Human Studies.

This system of relationship evaluation is down-to-earth, yet has complex and far-reaching applications. It can be used in simple situations, or applied to incredibly complex relationships. It is easy to learn, cross-cultural, and systematic in that it will tie in all the true information and learning you already know about relationships.

I feel confident that when you apply these principles to your own life, this information will work for you in both a strong and positive way. How Relationships Work (HRW) is the foundation to study the vast subject of personal human relationships. Once given the keys it illustrates how any relationship can be defined and evaluated based on three parts you can easily recognize. As you begin using this system to understand How Relationships Work your relationships will begin to improve greatly. The problems you may be experiencing will become a thing of the past. You will learn how to determine the proper relationship "seesaw" you need to meet your needs. You will also be able to choose and assess the positive qualities in others that are needed to make your "seesaw" work. Finally, all the potential for success, happiness, and personal satisfaction promised by positive relationships will become a reality.

Enjoy your reading; the subject matter is fascinating because YOU and YOUR life are ultimately what this book is about. My goal is to explain the basic principles—the nuts and bolts—of How Relationships Work. My deepest desire is to help you understand and benefit from this knowledge I'm sharing.

HRW is not just some philosophical theory, however; it is a practical subject for which you need to allow plenty of lab time. I feel certain you will have many insightful moments as you discover and integrate the bits and pieces of this system that will make it real for you. I don't know everything about relationships, but I do know how they work. And now, so too, can you.

*P*art *O*ne: Intro

This book functions somewhat like a
mini-encyclopedia with 3 main parts.

Part One provides the "philosophy"
of How Relationships Work.

It outlines the HRW Analogy in abridged form
so you have a complete overview of the system
before digging into Part Two.

To learn How Relationships Work,
you must understand and be familiar
with all the terms and explanations
as described in Part One.

Part Two covers each of the
12 generic relationships in detail.

Part Three provides the Practical.

CHAPTER 1

Introducing How Relationships Work

Everyone wants to achieve certain goals in life. Each of us has secret desires and dreams that we feel will bring us happiness. Yet few of us stop to realize how much the achievement of our personal and professional goals is directly related to the quality and success of our human relationships. Our experience of fulfillment in life hinges on our ability to understand, create, and participate in positive human relationships.

Each day you are engaged in dozens of human relationships. Do you know how each one functions and which relationships are best-suited to meet your personal needs? Are you able to analyze which relationships, if any, are causing you problems, and why? Do you always choose positive partners and know the best circumstances in which to conduct your relationships? For these purposes and more, you need a practical system of straightforward information about relationships—How Relationships Work.

The study of HRW is an engaging one. You are about to explore the fundamental principles underlying all human relationships and learn how to apply them to your personal life. This chapter introduces you to the raw ingredients, the basic building blocks, the key components of human relationships.

You will learn how these elements create your personal relationships. Ultimately, the true subject matter of this book is you; your life, your personality, and how it all fits into the unique relationships we all share.

The Language of How Relationships Work

To attempt a system of analyzing human relationships would seem impossible to most people. The subject is too complex to be covered in only one book they would say. However, the reason they say this is because most people find their relationships too confusing and overwhelming. Even the scholars don't have a simple system that can be used to understand how relationships work. Yet relationships are only confusing because people do not understand the basic principles by which they function.

Initially, the study of HRW begins much like the study of a new language. You will learn some basic terms to clarify the principles of the system. As you become comfortable using these definitions (which are all in plain English, by the way), you will develop a clarity and personal understanding of your relationships that no one had thought possible.

Part I of this book introduces each element necessary to analyze and understand a human relationship. Part II demonstrates how each element applies to each relationship. Part III gives you the tools to take these generic principles and integrate them into your personal relationships. Let's get started with some basic definitions and guidelines used throughout the book.

What Relationships Do We Study In HRW?

How Relationships Work divides what we call the "personal" human relationships into three main sections: Family, Social, and Work. A personal relationship is one in which there are only two people, not a group. There are 12 classic personal relationships.

FAMILY Relationships are determined by blood and contain distinct interactions that involve you and your family members. They are:

- Parent/Child Relationships
- Sibling/Sibling Relationships
- Grandparent/Grandchild Relationships

- Kin/Kin Relationships
- Adult Child/Parent Relationships

SOCIAL Relationships involve people in your life other than blood relatives in activities that usually do not involve the exchange of money. Included here are interactions with your friends, neighbors, and in-laws as well as relationships with members of the opposite sex. These are:

- Friend/Friend Relationships
- Boyfriend/Girlfriend Relationships
- Husband/Wife Relationships
- In-law/In-law Relationships
- Neighbor/Neighbor Relationships

WORK Relationships involve providing of goods and services together with other people. They include:

- Boss/Employee Relationships
- Coworker/Coworker Relationships

A fourth category of **Professional Relationships** is where you would place those relationships that provide a professional service to a client, patient, or customer. These relationships are not included as part of the primary 12 generic relationships; however, they function in the same way. Some examples are:

- Teacher/Student Relationships
- Doctor/Patient Relationships
- Lawyer/Client Relationships
- Priest/Parishioner Relationships
- Mechanic/Customer Relationships
- Policeman/Citizen Relationships

Just learning to categorize each of your primary human relationships into one of these first three groupings represents a significant step toward discussing them. Although each specific relationship will eventually be outlined in Part II, let's next introduce another basic concept of How Relationships Work.

What Do I Mean By The Term Generic?

The term *generic* defines the basic elements of a person, place, or thing without a brand-name identity. For example, butter is basically butter. Although many brands of butter are marketed with specialized packaging and advertising, they are each essentially the same—basic butter. There is only one major difference; brand names invariably cost more than generic brands due to the extra costs of marketing. If you purchase the inexpensive "plain-wrap" or "generic" brand of butter, you will be getting essentially the same product as the more expensive "brand" name.

Another aspect of what I mean by "generic" is that any product may be defined by its generic attributes and function. For example, what are the qualities of a generic car? At the very least, it has four wheels, a motor, a transmission, and a steering wheel. The purpose of a car is to transport yourself somewhere. Every car has these basic parts to provide that purpose. It is only the accessories, the advertising, and the brand name that separates one generic car from another.

How Relationships Work represents the compilation and distillation of numerous complex beliefs and principles associated with brand-name schools of philosophical, psychological, or religious thought. As a result, you won't have to study 1,000 different disciplines to learn the basic facts about human relationships. How Relationships Work will teach you all the core information related to the 12 personal human relationships without complicated packaging, marketing, or pricing.

In fact, you must be careful not to underestimate the value of How Relationships Work. Because it is *not* accompanied by hoopla and high prices, you might be tempted to think that it could not have much to offer. However, HRW offers more knowledge about relationships than all the high-priced philosophies and seminars combined precisely because there is *no* dogma or party line that must be followed. Also, many of the insights that HRW provides are available nowhere else because examining relationships from a generic perspective is, in itself, a new concept.

It can be fairly stated that nowhere else—not in any college or university, nor psychological seminar or religious institution, will you find the practical knowledge and understanding of human relationships that you will discover in How Relationships Work. Give this system a fair trial and see if you don't agree.

How Do I Define A Relationship?

In HRW, a relationship is defined as a dynamic interaction involving three distinct relationship elements. Although different from each other, each element is absolutely required to create the instance of the relationship.

Learning how these elements interact is the key to understanding your personal relationships. In its simplest form, all relationships take place:

- IN an Environment
- ON a Structure
- BETWEEN Two Co-partners

As you learn how these elements of Environment, Structure, and Two Co-partners interact with each other, you will begin to understand your personal relationships more clearly. The only thing keeping you from understanding your relationships right now is that you do not consciously know how these three elements function to create "a relationship." Because all human relationships must contain these three elements, these terms will help you clarify and understand large amounts of information about relationships in a manageable way.

Learning to understand how your relationships work, generically speaking, will teach you how to improve your personal relationships as well as provide you with the tools and understanding to make it happen. This body of information contained in the study of How Relationships Work is of the highest importance— both personally, in your daily life; and globally, in our future as a society.

What You Have Learned In Chapter One

There are three main categories of human relationships:

- Family
- Social
- Work

The generic Family Relationships are:

- Parent/Child Relationships
- Sibling/Sibling Relationships
- Grandparent/Grandchild Relationships
- Kin/Kin Relationships
- Adult Child/Parent Relationships

The generic Social Relationships are:

- Friend/Friend Relationships
- Boyfriend/Girlfriend Relationships
- Husband/Wife Relationships
- In-law/In-law Relationships
- Neighbor/Neighbor Relationships

The generic Work Relationships are:

- Boss/Employee Relationships
- Coworker/Coworker Relationships
- Professional Services Relationships (various types)
- Teacher/Student Relationships
- Doctor/Patient Relationships

Every generic relationship has three elements:

- An Environment
- A Structure
- Two Co-partners

CHAPTER 2

The HRW Playground Analogy

Imagine strolling through a park along a gentle path. On a grassy area in the middle of a playground, you notice an empty seesaw. As you pass by the seesaw, you think to yourself, "Gee, I'd like to go for a ride."

So you walk over and take a seat. At first, you sit on the low side and wait for a few minutes, but you don't seem to be getting anywhere!

After a few minutes you get bored, note the high side, and think, "Yes, that's where I want to be!" So you walk around and climb up on the high side. Before long (crash!), you find yourself, once again, on the low side wondering why you aren't having any fun.

If you are clever, motivated, and have the time, you might work out some alternative ways to ride the seesaw, such as filling a bag with sand approximately your own weight, balancing it on one side, and climbing up on the other end. You might also sit on one end of the seesaw and ask people walking by to ride with you. You could be successful if you were lucky enough to meet a like-minded individual also wanting a seesaw ride.

On the other hand, you might be disappointed to discover that most people passing by did not have the time, did not know how to ride, or were simply too afraid to try because they had been hurt on seesaw rides before.

What Is the HRW Playground Analogy?

The HRW Playground Analogy will be your constant friend while learning the language and concepts of How Relationships Work. Your intuitive understanding of the parts of a children's playground will help you to easily visualize and clarify the three basic elements of any human relationship. It is amazing how much you already know, even if you have never studied relationships before!

Everyone seems to know the answer to the following question:

"What are the basic aspects of a children's playground?"

Given enough time, people always describe in one form or another the following three elements:

The Play Area

The first element people observe is that the playground is in a physical setting. This could be a park, a yard area, or an open field. Naturally, there needs to be a defined area where the playground structures, such as swings, slides, and merry-go-rounds are located so the children can play.

Playground "Structures"

The second element people usually mention is that the playground must have different structures within the park. Swings, slides, and merry-go-rounds provide the equipment upon which the children play. For example, the seesaw is a structure: a thick plank placed across a base or fulcrum. Without a board to sit on, there is no mechanism for the children to ride.

Children Playing

The final element always mentioned is the children themselves. After all, what is a playground without children? They are the ones who come to the park and enjoy playing on the equipment. Without the children, all you have is a field with rusting structures.

As you can see, it is a simple matter to describe a generic playground: it will have a play area, some structures, and playing children. People always define these three elements as being part of a generic playground. This holds true whether the playground is Central Park in New York City, at Golden Gate Park in San Francisco, or The Domain in Sydney, Australia.

If there was ever a book called *The Great Playgrounds of the World*, it would include a collection of the most famous of the "brand-name" parks. They might have breathtaking environments or extraordinary equipment on which the children can play. But for all their diversity and uniqueness, each playground always needs to contain these same three elements: an environment, various structures, and children.

The HRW Playground Analogy is used to help you remember that all human relationships have the same three basic elements. They always take place IN an Environment, ON a seesaw Structure, and BETWEEN Two Co-Partners. Without each of these elements, a relationship would be unable to function. In fact, there would be no relationship at all.

Why the HRW Playground Analogy?

The hardest part about evaluating your relationships is to remember that all your relationships consist of only three basic elements: an Environment, a Structure, and Two Co-partners. It helps you to remember these three elements more easily by using an analogy. Knowing the HRW Playground Analogy enables you to quickly recall the three elements when you are "out on the street."

How Relationships Work is really a book about ideal generic relationships. However I'm guessing that what you really want is to learn more about your *personal* relationships. Your *personal* relationships take place "out on the street" in the "real world." You will need to access this HRW information many times throughout the day, and it isn't practical to carry this book everywhere you go. The HRW Playground Analogy gives you an easy way to remember the three elements of any relationship, even your personal ones. It functions as a simple memory key you can refer to it as many times a day as you need to focus your knowledge of HRW.

The best part is that the HRW Playground Analogy correlates directly to your personal experience in human relationships. Here is how:

An Environment

Every relationship you have takes place in an Environment. There must be a place or location where you and your Co-partner interact. Simply said, this is the Environment.

A Seesaw Structure

Every relationship you are in takes place on a structural platform. In HRW, the seesaw (also teeter-totter) is used to represent this relationship structure.

A seesaw is a physical platform upon which two people, one on either end, ride together. In the same way, your relational structure functions like a seesaw platform upon which the dynamics of the relationship depend.

As such, it is an external "reality," or agreed-upon set of dynamics, created by our combined humanity that we humans have agreed to as being the standard of our relations. Although every relationship has a different structure, each is similar in that it is based on a seesaw.

For example, three different relationship structures are the:

- Parent/Child Structure
- Friend/Friend Structure
- Boss/Employee Structure

Although each of these relational structures is distinctly differ- ent, they each *function* like a seesaw. The key thing to remember about a relationship seesaw is that it is a neutral platform upon which the two riders sit. It is not part of the riders themselves.

Two Co-partners

Two people represent the third essential element a relationship requires to exist. One person alone cannot make a relationship (seesaw) function properly. Only when both people are seated equally on opposite ends does a relationship (seesaw) have the potential to perform as it should.

In HRW the term *Co-partner* describes the two people riding on the relationship seesaw. Without two "Co-partners," the rela- tionship simply will not work. Although there may be a playground (the Environment) and a seesaw (the Structure), there can be no activity in a relationship without the Two Co-partners (children to play).

So, for the most fun and the best results, the action of a rela- tionship must take place in a safe and supportive ENVIRONMENT, on a sturdy and well-defined seesaw STRUCTURE, between TWO CO-PARTNERS who are both on the same seesaw. As you shall more fully discover in the chapters ahead, these three elements provide the foundation for all positive and successful relationships.

What You Have Learned In Chapter Two

The HRW Playground Analogy: a children's playground contains three elements:

- – A place to play
- – Structures
- – Children playing

This translates directly into the three elements of any generic relationship:

- – An Environment
- – A Seesaw Structure
- – Two Co-partners on the same seesaw

The Three Elements of the HRW Playground Analogy

In this chapter, we are going to examine each element in more detail as well as do some practical work. But first, let's review each element once again.

In an Environment

The ENVIRONMENT is the physical setting and circumstances surrounding the interaction of a relationship. Every relationship takes place in a specific environment. This environment may have a major or a minor influence on the relationship, but it will always be a factor. In the HRW Playground Analogy, the environment is the park area of the children's playground. It is the external surroundings in which a relationship takes place.

On a Structure

The seesaw STRUCTURE represents the platform upon which the relationship is based. Without a Structure, the relationship has no basis and cannot exist. In the HRW Playground Analogy, the structure of a relationship is represented by a seesaw. It is separate and distinct from the Environment and/or the Two Co-partners.

Between Two Co-partners

The TWO CO-PARTNERS create a unique dynamic tension by interacting on the relationship Structure. According to the HRW Playground Analogy, if only one person is on a seesaw, he or she will be unable to make it function properly. In the same way, if only one person is on a relationship Structure, he or she will be unable to fulfill the potential of the relationship. This is why two people are required to establish the third relational element; one person on either side.

"Out On the Street"

Be also aware that the purpose of this book is to help you integrate the concepts of HRW "out on the street." You are not just reading about relationships for your entertainment. You want help and practical ideas to make your personal relationships function more smoothly. Your understanding of HRW will be based on your knowledge of each element as discussed. Each aspect of a relationship has key features that will enable you to diagnose problem areas.

Your relationships take place "out on the street." Even though you are reading about relationships right now, this information will not help you until it is applied in the "real world." This is where and when you will need this information.

The following section is designed to help you to begin to think in How Relationships Work terms so that you will have access to the information where and when you need it.

Special Caution: Do not write your answers down; do these exercises mentally, inside your mind. By doing these exercises as you read, you will be practicing the mental ways in which you will access these principles "out on the street." Although they may seem difficult at first, as you begin "thinking generic," you will find the answers come easier with each question.

What You Should Know By Chapter Three

What three Types categorize all human relationships?

- 1. _____
- 2. _____
- 3. _____

What are the 12 categories of generic human relationships?

- _____
- 1. _____/_____
- 2. _____/_____
- 3. _____/_____
- 4. _____/_____
- 5. _____/_____
- _____
- 6. _____/_____
- 7. _____/_____
- 8. _____/_____
- 9. _____/_____
- 10. _____/_____
- _____
- 11. _____/_____
- 12 _____/_____

What three parts are generic to any human relationship?

- 1. _____
- 2. _____
- 3. _____

The next three chapters will specifically examine each element of a generic relationship (Environment, Structure, and Two Co-partners) in more detail. It turns out that each of the three primary elements has three subparts which combine to create each element.

CHAPTER 4

*M*ore about the Environment

The Environment is a crucial aspect in any relationship because it forms the background against which the overall interaction takes place. The Environment may be an integral part of the relationship interaction or simply a backdrop for the interaction between Co-partners. The Environment can help, hurt, or simply be neutral as far as its effect on a relationship. If the Environment is hostile, however, a relationship will be very difficult.

For example, the interaction of a Doctor/Patient Relationship could occur in many Environments, the obvious choices being a doctor's clinic or a hospital. However, the same relationship could take place in the Environment of a battlefield during a war. In this situation, the Environment would contribute considerable tension and urgency to the interaction.

The Boyfriend/Girlfriend Relationship could take place against the neutral backdrop of New York City; Venice, Italy; or Sydney, Australia. Yet, if the interaction took place inside a prison, the Environment would be a more critical factor in the relationship.

Another case in which the Environment is the main cause of relationship problems is when the Two Co-partners are separated by great distance. In this situation, there is too much Environment. An example might be a Husband/Wife Relationship where both Co-partners normally live in Los Angeles but one Co-partner is obligated to spend two weeks of every month in England. Although the Structure and the Two Co-partners may be positive in nature, the relationship will suffer considerable tension due to excess Environment.

The Environment is often the initiating factor in a relationship. For example, you might meet another player on the squash courts and establish a Friend/Friend Relationship. Or, the fact that you live in a certain neighborhood (Environment) automatically means you will meet more people from that neighborhood.

Another example of the Environment's influence can be seen in the Boss/Employee Relationship. Suppose your desk at work is in the office next door to your Boss. Then imagine that your desk is located two buildings away from your boss. Naturally, this distance, or change in environment, would create a different feeling regarding your Boss/Employee Relationship. This illustrates how your relationship could be negatively or positively influenced by the physical circumstances (Environment) of your work place.

Every Environment has three components. They are:

- The Location (in which the relationship takes place)
- The Duration (how long both Co-partners have been on the relationship structure)
- The Timing (the time of day and the number of times of the relationship interaction)

❶ LOCATION

Location refers to the physical boundaries and conditions surrounding the relationship interaction. Basically, this means: How far can you see around you? Do you see four walls, wide open spaces, or the inside of a car? Where is the action of your relationship taking place? What are the circumstances of your Environment? Are you in a foxhole with hand grenades bursting around you? Or is your relationship taking place in a restaurant while sipping wine?

The location of an Environment and the particular features associated with this Environment can play an important role in determining the positive or negative qualities of your relationships. Many people have been involved in a wonderful relationship, only to have some aspect of the Environment change, which made the relationship impossible to continue.

❷ DURATION

Duration refers to the total length of time you and your Co-partner have spent interacting on a relationship structure. In other words, how long have both of you been sitting on your relationship seesaw? All relationships have a beginning, a middle, and an end. Some types of relationships, such as the Clerk/Customer Relationship, may only last a few minutes; others, such as the Sibling/Sibling Relationship, may last many decades.

Duration also refers to the length of interaction of the relationship. For example, suppose you met your current girlfriend or boyfriend four years ago. This provides some clues as to certain aspects of your relationship interaction. On the other hand, what kinds of dynamics are suggested if you met your current girlfriend or boyfriend just four days ago?

❸ TIMING

Timing refers to the time of day the relationship interaction takes place. For example, the timing for jogging alone in Central Park would be quite different for a single female at 10 o'clock in the morning as opposed to 10 o'clock at night. Most work relationships take place in a daytime Environment. However, a significant number of work relationships have timing that occurs at night, which could have a significant impact on the stresses and strains of the job. The Timing of the relationship interaction is often a critical factor in the experience of that relationship.

Timing also refers to the length of time you spend interacting with your Co-partner. Suppose you are the son or daughter in a Parent/Child Relationship, and you interact with your father off and on for 20 minutes to two hours each day. This implies one set of values reflecting the quality of your relationship that most people would consider characteristic of a Parent/Child relationship.

How would this compare to the same relationship seesaw (Parent/Child) with your father if the timing of your interaction is only two days in a row every second week? In this relationship, the Environmental factor of Timing would have a key impact which most people would immediately understand.

Timing is also a factor in the number of times you interact with your Co-partner over a set period of time. Is your Timing three times in three weeks or three times in three years?

What You Have Learned In Chapter Four

Every Environment has three components. Each component of the Environment is important to the positive functioning of a relationship. They are:

- The Location (in which the relationship takes place)
- The Duration (how long both Co-partners have been in the relationship structure)
- Timing (the time of day and number of times of the relationship interaction)

The Environment of each relationship we have can affect our relationships tremendously. Although the Environmental element of a relationship is usually easy to determine, many people never stop to consider the positive or negative influences it can have.

Positive relationships typically take place in an Environment that is nurturing and supportive of the relationship. They occur in an Environment that has a supportive **Location**, over a **Duration** necessary to support the needs and goals of the Two Co-partners, and with a **Timing** (both in frequency and time of day) that is generically appropriate for the relationship interaction.

CHAPTER 5

*M*ore about the Structure

The second element that all relationships share is the Structure upon which the Two Co-partners interact. Without the seesaw Structure, the relationship could not exist. Each relationship Structure has three essential components; without which the Structure is incomplete. They are:

- Roles
- Rules
- Customs

❹ ROLES

Roles are the designated parts that each Co-partner will play on his/her side of the seesaw structure. Your understanding of this component of How Relationships Work is crucial. A Role is not the particular individual in a relationship, but rather an innate aspect of the relationship Structure. The Structure of a Husband/Wife Relationship contains the Husband Role and the Wife Role. The Parent/Child Relationship has the Parent Role and the Child Role associated with its seesaw structure.

A Role summarizes specific duties associated with the relationship. Roles exist as part of the seesaw structure and always contain two generic Roles; one for each side of the seesaw. Roles may be identical in a relationship, such as in Friend/Friend Relationships, or they may be quite different, as in the Boss/Employee Relationship. Some Roles imply a variety of obligations associated with their performance. Others may have very limited assignments.

Roles reflect a job to be done. They involve a set of responsibilities specifically associated with that Role. Roles are comparable to a job description for employment in that they specify the actions in a relationship. Roles guide a person toward the behavior expected when participating in a relationship. Every Role has a set of established behaviors associated with its side of the relationship Structure.

To achieve a successful relationship, each Co-partner must choose a Role in the relationship Structure and stick to that Role. If both people try to sit on the same side of a seesaw, what happens? If both Co-partners in a relationship try to play the same Role, the same thing will happen to their relationship. By definition, the Structure of a relationship is based on two people assuming the opposite Roles on a relationship seesaw.

For example, in the Boss and Employee Structure, each Co-partner has a specific Role. If both Co-partners on the seesaw attempt to play the Boss Role, this will cause stress and friction because the duties of the Employee will not be performed. Similarly, if the person playing the Boss Role does not take the responsibility to manage and delegate the workload, then the relationship will suffer because the Employee will have no direction. Neither person in the relationship will get their needs met if either person is not fulfilling his/her Role.

Roles Define the Relationship

Roles also define a relationship. They give the relationship Structure its name, and they provide a blueprint for the characteristic social behaviors associated with each relationship. The various combinations of Roles identify the type of relationship Structure.

For example, the seesaw Structure of a Husband/Wife relationship is distinguished from that of the Boss/Employee relationship only by the function of the different Roles. The same two people may be involved in both relationships. Yet, since the Roles (jobs to be done) for each relationship are different, the dynamics of the interaction between the Co-partners are also different.

Furthermore, it must be noted that Roles only exist in relationship to each other. For example, there is no such entity as a Husband/Employee relationship because the two Roles together are incongruent.

Roles and Accountability

Roles also establish guidelines for accountability when evaluating relationships. The playing of a relationship Role reflects a skill by which each person may be objectively evaluated.

Ideally, each Co-partner in a relationship is aware of the expected social behavior associated with his/her Role. Whether they are aware of this or not, both Co-partners in a relationship will be evaluated by the other as to how well they play their Role. The interesting part is that he/she must judge the person, not the Role.

If an actor playing Hamlet does a terrible job, critics don't blame the role of Hamlet; they blame the actor playing that Role. If a person playing the Boss Role does a terrible job, the employees should be blaming the *person* playing the Boss Role, not the Role itself.

With respect to HRW, many people have a muddled perception of their Roles in various relationships. They often try to avoid some aspect of their Role or attempt to play the Role assigned to their Co-partner. They may never have had a healthy model on which to base the performance of a Role in a relationship. Due to bad experiences with negative Co-partners, some people hate a particular Role so much that they have trouble with any person in a relationship playing that role. Whatever the reason, this lack of clarity between the Roles vs. the Co-partners in a relationship has a negative impact on many relationships.

By learning the generic behaviors expected of each Role in a relationship and by evaluating both yourself and your Co-partner according to these guidelines, you will become more attuned to the difference between Roles and Co-partners in your personal relationships.

❺ RULES

Rules are the specific instructions that go with each relationship role. Rules provide the quickest, easiest, and most effective ways of performing the duties associated with a role. Rules may be explicit or implied, but Rules are always part of a relationship's Structure.

Rules suggest appropriate behavior for the conduct of each Role. Knowing and following the Rules of each relationship is a specific key to more effective relationship skills. Following the Rules builds the value of a relationship. Breaking the Rules destroys the value of a relationship.

The importance of Rules is that they protect both sides in a relationship Structure. Rules set guidelines for permissible and non-permissible behavior and provide socially sanctioned protection without each person having to specifically request it. This enables each person in the relationship to enjoy a sense of personal security while performing his/her Role.

Not only do Rules ensure that relationship goals can be attained, they also help you avoid common difficulties associated with a relationship. Some Rules have been formalized to the point of becoming legalized sanctions. Other Rules are more informal, reflecting cultural influences, although breaking these rules still results in significant social penalties.

How Rules Developed

Rules reflect the behaviors that most people in society find socially appropriate within the context of a relationship. They developed from tribal social mores and became established in human society through precedent. Rules are biologically and socially inspired and are taught to us through social assimilation. Although relationship Rules may vary slightly from culture to culture, there is a consensus on Rules governing each generic human relationship.

Each relationship has many Rules. While they may be unwritten, the Rules exist as common beliefs or shared opinions as to what is or is not acceptable conduct for people playing the Roles in a relationship. Even if the relationship Rules are unwritten, they are still in force.

We are not formally taught the Rules of relationships. We learn them through example and through emulation of our role models. If we are exposed to negative or unhealthy relationships, we will learn a set of Rules that function negatively when we apply them.

HRW helps you more clearly identify the positive Rules associated with each Role in a generic relationship. You can then use this information to evaluate and enhance your personal relationships.

Types of Rules

There can be many rules for a relationship's role; as many as 40 or more sometimes. One way to recall or think about rules is to determine which of four possible types of rules you want to consider. These four types are:

- Physical
- Emotional
- Mental
- Social

When you list the rules for each role in this way, it's very easy to keep track of a large number of rules.

Customs

Customs, the third component of a relationship Structure, reflect the cultural, religious, and political manners associated with a relationship. They are non-essential behaviors that accompany the interaction within specific relationships. They are part of the relationship Structure in conjunction with the established cultural, religious, and political practices of a particular society.

Customs cannot be generic

Customs cannot be generic. It's impossible! A custom is by definition non-generic; this is precisely why it's called a Custom! So, why are Customs a part of HRW? How do Customs fit into a system for defining relationships, generically speaking?

Customs are an integral part of How Relationships Work because customs vary so widely among all human cultures, we need a place to make note of them. In fact, every human society will have cultural, religious, and political differences associated with the twelve generic human relationships.

Although Customs are not absolutely required for the existence of a relationship, if they are ignored or omitted within a certain culture, people from this culture will feel offended. Customs provide emotional comfort that nurtures and gladdens the participants in a relationship. By retaining the Customs associated with a generic relationship, members of society thereby experience a reassuring sense of belonging and community.

Cultural Customs

Cultural Customs typically reflect the country where you were born and/or the language you learned while growing up. For example, you may have grown up in Italy, in which case you are culturally Italian. If you were born in El Salvador, culturally you would be considered Spanish. If you were born to 100% Lebanese parents but were brought up in Australia, you will experience certain cultural conflicts.

Although every relationship Structure has Customs, the specific Customs will vary according to your circumstances. Each society has its own set of Customs that accompanies the twelve generic relationships. Some things that are defined by customs are the use of language, distinctions of social class, and urban lifestyles. The influence of customs complements, rather than alters, the function of generic relationships.

Religious Customs

Religious Customs clearly are part of your family's chosen religion. For example, all religions recognize some type of marriage ceremony which establishes the Husband/Wife Relationship as a generic relationship. Whether the members of one religion jump over a stick to proclaim their marriage or walk under an arch, this specific behavior reflects a Custom.

Political Customs

Each country (and thus it's set of laws and political system) has its own perspective on itself as a global participant. It would not be a country if something specific to its creation did not make it unique; otherwise, it would be part of another country. Each country's Customs gain importance through historical precedent. At one time the oft repeated actions associated with a particular relationship may have had a purpose which practicality has long since passed.

The transfer of Customs is a developmental process through which the children in a culture gradually absorb the patterns of behavior (norms, values, and cultural heritage) presented by the majority of people living in their society. While this process of socialization occurs most strongly in childhood and adolescence, it continues throughout the human life span.

The fact that various human societies have different customs does not change the generic nature of relationships. As a key component of the relationship Structure, Political Customs account for the political differences between societies possessing identical generic relationships.

What You Have Learned In Chapter Five

The Structure of a relationship contains three components. They are:

- Roles
- Rules
- Customs

Roles are the part each Co-partner plays in the relationship Structure. The vast complexity of a Role in a relationship can be broken down into four categories:

- Physical
- Emotional
- Mental
- Social

Rules are the specific behaviors that guide the performance of a Role. The sheer number of Rules for the various roles can be more easily managed but placing them into one of four major categories:

- Physical
- Emotional
- Mental
- Social

Customs are the cultural, religious, and political behaviors that accompany a generic relationship. If you need to discuss and assign a specific custom to a particular relationship, it is helpful to use the categories of:

- Cultural
- Religious
- Political

CHAPTER 6

*M*ore about the Two Co-partners

The third element of any generic relationship is always known as the Two Co-partners. The Two Co-partners are the individual humans acting in the roles of the relationship. As you remember from the HRW Playground Analogy, if only one person attempts to operate a seesaw, he/she will have some serious problems. Each relationship requires two people to "ride" or play the generic roles of the relationship. This is why it takes a combination of two people to make up the third and final element of a generic relationship; one person is simply not enough.

The interaction between Two Co-partners on a relationship seesaw initiates a dynamic exchange which creates the unique experience of their relationship. The individual energies of the Two Co-partners bring a unique quality and essence to the generic seesaw structure that only those two people share.

In terms or How Relationships Work, each Co-partner can be objectively evaluated based on three separate components:

- Traits
- Needs
- Tactics

❼ TRAITS

Traits are the characteristics of a Co-partner's personality relevant to his/her participation in relationships. Although each person has many personality traits, HRW is concerned with seven Traits that specifically apply to the functioning of a relationship.

The seven personal Traits which HRW identifies as specifically important to relationship interactions are:

- Being Attracted
- Being Committed
- Being Genuine
- Being Trustworthy
- Being Emotionally Mature
- Having Communication Skills
- Having Problem-Solving Skills

Co-partners energize a relationship Structure with the vitality reflecting these Traits. The seven positive Traits of a Co-partner will enhance any relationship structure; conversely, the seven negative Traits of a Co-partner will sabotage any relationship structure. The success or failure of a relationship depends heavily on the combined Traits of the Two Co-partners.

Being Attracted

Being Attracted is a strong feeling or sense of connection with your Co-partner. Without a solid attraction, Two Co-partners will be unable to sustain their relationship because neither of them will "stay on the seesaw."

Ideally, both Co-partners feel this sense of connection. If one of the participants on the relationship seesaw is lacking this Trait, the relationship will be too one-sided to succeed.

Different relationship Structures have different qualities of Being Attracted between Co-partners. For example, in Family Relationships, the attraction is based upon blood and family ties. In Social Relationships, the attraction is based upon mutual admiration and sharing. In Work Relationships, the attraction is based on financial needs or similar creative interests.

Being Committed

Being Committed is the measure of each Co-partner's willingness to invest time and energy into the relationship Structure as well as the guarantee each Co-partner gives the other that he/she will remain "on the seesaw." Both Co-partners want to feel secure about investing time and energy in a relationship that is critical to their future happiness.

Another aspect of Being Committed is the motivation each Co-partner has to meet each other's needs. If only one Co-partner acts to meet the needs of the other, the long-term value of the relationship will suffer. Each Co-partner has a finite amount of energy. Because he or she is involved in many other relationships, there is only so much energy to go around. Therefore, each Co-partner's ability to apportion Commitment to a personal relationship is a crucial test of his/her relationship skills.

Ideally, each Co-partner contributes a balanced amount of time and energy (Commitment) to their relationship, although this energy may assume different forms. For example, in a Work Relationship, one Co-partner might put in 90 percent of the time and the other might contribute 90 percent of the money, but the contribution of energy would be considered "balanced" by both sides.

If one Co-partner puts in a disproportionate amount of time or energy, the relationship will be imbalanced, thus creating instability. Referencing the HRW Playground Analogy, if one person on the seesaw tries to do all the work for both sides, the results cannot be successful. Even if one person is 100% committed to the relationship from his/her side, without the same from the other person, the relationship won't succeed.

Being Genuine

Being Genuine is the willingness and honesty that each Co-partner has to reveal his/her true thoughts, feelings, and needs.

Being Genuine in relationships is appreciated by other genuine Co-partners more than any other quality.

Co-partners must be willing to be honest with one another. If one Co-partner tries to camouflage his/her true thoughts, feelings, or needs, the relationship will only suffer. If the Co-partners conceal their thoughts, feelings, or needs from each other, the relationship can be only superficial, at best. If you or your Co-partner express opinions or values that are false, your relationship may continue, but it will be based on pretense.

Genuine Co-partners do not hide their thoughts, feelings, or needs; nor will they expend energy building facades. They are not evasive in conversation nor do they distort the facts about their job, accomplishments, income, age, marital status, or other aspects of their life.

Being Genuine means that you will reveal information about yourself within a proper context. Relationships have appropriate times and methods for self-disclosure. By following the correct guidelines for self-disclosure, you will protect your emotions from being hurt by others.

Being Trustworthy

Being Trustworthy is the ability to depend upon your Co-partner as well as he/she being able to depend on you. This Trait gives your Co-partner the foundation for building trust, which is an essential aspect of exchanging needs. If you don't trust your Co-partner on your relationship seesaw, how relaxed and comfortable will you feel riding it with them? Can you truly trust that they won't abruptly jump off the seesaw and leave you crashing to the ground? The betrayal of trust between Co-partners is the bane of all relationships.

Trustworthy Co-partners will not reveal information given in confidence nor later use this information against you. Nor do they criticize each other in public. Once trust is established, Co-partners will be open and honest about any condition or fact in their lives. The Roles of every relationship benefit when both Co-partners are trustworthy.

Being Emotionally Mature

Being Emotionally Mature is the ability of each Co-partner to balance his/her reasonable and realistic needs against the needs of the Co-partner. If either Co-partner is immature, their overriding concern for meeting their own needs will hurt the relationship over the long term. An immature Co-partner could also deny his/her own needs in deference to his/her Co-partner, which has the same end result of a dysfunctional relationship.

Emotionally Mature Co-partners maintain a balanced perspective of needs within a relationship. They understand their own needs and motives and are conversely aware of and sensitive to the needs and motives of their Co-partners. They recognize the importance of a relationship's structure and concentrate upon nurturing and protecting it. They also reject the formation of relationships with Co-partners who appear to have negative Traits.

Emotionally Mature Co-partners have a positive sense of self-esteem which includes self-caring and self-sufficiency. Because they recognize and understand their priorities, they use their energy and skills in a positive and fulfilling manner. Emotionally Mature Co-partners are interested and invested in enjoying and improving their relationships. They know how important relationships are to their personal happiness. Thus, they will expend energy to achieve this purpose.

Having Communication Skills

Having Communication Skills is a much-desired trait in a Co-partner's personality. Everyone feels and has needs, but this does not necessarily mean they are communicating them properly to others. A Co-partner must be able to accurately communicate what he/she thinking, feeling, and truly needing to their Co-partner.

The other Co-partner must then be able to receive the communication in the way it was intended and have the proper communication skills to craft a reply. This will keep the relationship working on a positive level to avoid problems. Having Communication Skills is a major necessity for maintaining positive relationships.

Having Problem-Solving Skills

Having Problem-Solving Skills means being willing and able to resolve problems within a relationship. Relationships are a union, and unresolved conflict will cause the union to weaken. Since no relationship can be without conflict, these skills are essential for a relationship to run smoothly. The style used by the Two Co-partners to solve problems determines the quality of the relationship.

Co-partners with positive Traits realize that most problems in a relationship are created by unmet needs. They understand that the way to avoid problems is to communicate honestly and openly on a regular basis with their Co-partners. But, if a problem does escalate to become a suppressed issue of the relationship interaction, then Problem-Solving Skills become very important for the survival of the relationship.

An attracted, committed, genuine, trustworthy, and emotionally mature Co-partner who has positive communication and problem-solving skills will be accountable for every relationship he/she enters. Even if the relationship must end, a Co-partner with positive Traits will minimize the harmful emotional and psychological effects.

❽ NEEDS

Co-partners' needs propel them toward specific relationships and provide the motivation to actively participate in a relationship. Each Co-partner brings a personal set of Needs to the relationship. The desire to meet his/her Needs is the reason the individual enters a relationship in the first place.

Each type of relationship meets a generic set of Needs. Ideally, each Co-partner chooses the generic relationship structure which best fulfills the personal Needs he or she wants to fulfill. For example, if you took a group of strangers whose Needs were precisely known and grouped them together on a remote island, you would be able to unerringly pick the types of relationships they would form and with whom.

The worst possible outcome of a relationship is the failure to meet your Needs. Being passive or submissive about meeting your own Needs hurts both people. It hurts you because you are not getting what you need and want, and it hurts your Co-partner because he/she is unable to make you happy.

If you are unable or unwilling to communicate your Needs, you're essentially cheating yourself by precluding the possibility of having your Needs met. As a matter of reciprocity, your function in a relationship is to meet the needs of your Co-partner, whatever they may be.

Needs are categorized into four categories. Learning to use these categories to identify your Needs will save you hours of wasted time trying to determine that too-often-unidentifiable "what is missing" element in your relationships. They are:

- Physical
- Emotional
- Mental
- Social

Physical Needs (P)

Physical Needs are those that involve the corporeal body and physiological processes. Eating, drinking, and sleeping are some examples of Physical Needs. We also obviously need shelter and clothing to protect us from the environment.

Emotional Needs (E)

Emotional Needs are those that involve the giving and receiving of emotions and feelings between Co-partners. Being loved, accepted, and nurtured are some examples of Emotional Needs. These needs would normally be associated with the Inner Child in Self-Parenting terms.

Mental Needs (M)

Mental Needs are those that involve thinking and logic. Curiosity, desire to learn, and exploration of new ideas are some examples of Mental Needs. These needs are typically motivated by the ego or what we call the Inner Parent in Self-Parenting terms.

Social Needs (S)

Social Needs are those that involve interacting with other people in groups. In the HRW system Social Needs imply you and your Co-partner on your seesaw when relating to outside people or groups. Examples are sharing celebrations, holidays, and relating to members of the public.

However, much of HRW is devoted to helping YOU understand your Needs on *your* side of the seesaw and teaching you to choose the best relationships to meet your various PEMS Needs.

In Part II of this book, each generic relationship will be outlined according to the Needs of each Co-partner.

❾ TACTICS

Tactics, the third and final component of the Two Co-partners, reflect the methods chosen by each Co-partner to meet his/her relationship needs. They represent strategic choices made from a range of rule-bound options.

Understanding the Roles and being aware of the Rules in a generic relationship do not fully explain the actions of your Co-partner. For example, you could be the runner in a race (your Role) and know the rules to win, but these two factors would not give you a method for winning the race (your need). Tactics are your plan of action based on a strategy to win the race.

Tactics: Positive or Negative

The Tactics chosen by each Co-partner in a relationship can generally be evaluated as positive or negative. Tactics that follow the rules are permitted and accepted as fair. Some Tactics are outside the rules of the relationship and are not allowed. For example, it was deemed unacceptable for runners to choose the tactics of taking the subway in their quest to win the New York Marathon.

Other tactical behavior might be considered acceptable within the Rules, but ineffective or impractical in terms of meeting your Needs. For example, running backwards is a legal Tactic for running in a race, but it is not an effective way to win. Ideally, each Co-partner in a relationship would use Tactics that are effective and are within the rules.

The Tactics of each Co-partner are closely linked to his/her Traits. If a Co-partner uses negative Tactics to meet his/her needs in a relationship, then that person has negative Traits. Conversely, a person with negative traits will often choose negative tactics.

If a Co-partner uses positive Tactics to meet his/her needs within a relationship this typically means that person has positive Traits. Each Co-partner is assumed to have a combination of positive and negative Traits. Ideally, the Co-partners you choose for your relationships will have many more positive Traits than negative. However, one bad trait could overrule many "good" ones, so it's an ongoing evaluation you always have to monitor.

What You Have Learned In Chapter Six

You have learned that each Co-partner can be objectively evaluated in HRW terms based on three criteria:

–   Traits
–   Needs
–   Tactics

The seven Traits identified as particularly important to relationship interactions are:

–   Being Attracted
–   Being Committed
–   Being Genuine
–   Being Trustworthy
–   Being Emotionally Mature
–   Having Communication Skills
–   Having Problem-Solving Skills

The four categories of Needs (PEMS) are:

–   Physical Needs involving the body and physiology
–   Emotional Needs involving feelings
–   Mental Needs involving thinking and logic
–   Social Needs involving interacting with others from within your personal relationship

Tactics are the ways and means that each Co-partner uses to meet his/her needs and they can be evaluated as:

–   Positive.
–   Negative

Conclusion of Part One

Now you know the basic language of How Relationships Work. You know that all human relationships can be categorized using three major divisions: Family, Social, or Work.

You understand that each generic relationship has three major elements, without which it cannot exist: an Environment, its Structure, and Two Co-partners.

You also know that every element has three components.

- The Environment has:
    - Location
    - Timing
    - Duration
- The Structure has:
    - Roles
    - Rules
    - Customs
- The Two Co-partners have:
    - Traits
    - Needs
    - Tactics

Part Two of How Relationships Work will discuss each type of generic relationship in detail as well as offer specific descriptions of each relationship's major elements and subparts.

*P*art *T*wo: Intro

Part 2 provides specific details for
the 12 Generic Relationships
according to their 3 elements and
3-subparts as described in Part One.

They are listed here in order of importance
starting with the Family, going to the Social,
and then finishing with the Work.

These chapters are written so the ideal
"generic" relationship can be reviewed quickly.
They are here to jog your memory in
the correct area and be a source of reference.

Sometimes you don't know what's wrong in a
relationship until you find out what's right.

Explore Part Two chapters in any order you
wish. I'm guessing you might possibly be
thinking of going to the "relationship
for which you are having the most problems
right now" chapter.

It's completely up to you, the esteemed reader.

PART TWO: SECTION ONE

INTRO TO
FAMILY RELATIONSHIPS

CHAPTER 7

*T*he Parent/Child Relationship

The Parent/Child Relationship is the primary human relationship. As the first relationship experienced by a person entering the world, it establishes the foundation for all other relationships. Also, the experience each child has as a member of a Parent/Child Relationship becomes the basis for the parenting they give their own children. Thus, this relationship carries a multi-generational legacy.

During the early years of the relationship, generic parents have complete responsibility for the life of the child. Through the very nature of their role, parents are assigned all power and all knowledge. They serve as the complete source of survival for the child. Without parents or parental substitutes to love, protect, teach, guide, feed, supervise, and give affection, the child will die.

Parent/Child Environment

The Environment is the living situation in which the Parent/Child Relationship takes place.

❶ LOCATION

The Location of the Parent/Child Environment is the home. This includes all aspects of external family life such as:

- Parent and sibling interaction
- Providing food
- Cooking
- Eating
- Sleeping
- Communicating
- Leisure activities
- Sports
- Lessons
- Television

Other potential factors of the P/C location are:

- The room where the child sleeps
- The home address
- Local aspects of the neighborhood

The Location is any part of the Environment that surrounds the Parent/Child interaction. For example, the Location for a Parent/Child Relationship could be a circus, a freeway underpass, or various military bases. Other family conditions that are important aspects of Location that can affect the Parent/Child Relationship are:

- Health status of other family members
- How often the family has moved
- The parent's relationship

❷ DURATION

Technically, the Duration of the Parent/Child Relationship continues until the death of one of the Co-partners. This is because the Parent/Child Relationship is biologically based. As the saying goes, "You only have one set of parents."

Practically however, the Duration of the relationship continues only as long as both parent and child remain on the relationship seesaw. If either the parent or child abandons the structure for any reason, the relationship is functionally over.

❸ TIMING

Timing refers to the amount of time the Co-partners spend interacting. This may vary from a consistent hour every day (as long as both Co-partners are alive) to none at all if, for example, a parent dies or abandons the child after he/she is born.

The Timing of the Parent/Child Environment is typically 24 hours a day during the early years which gradually lessens as the child matures and becomes more independent.

In a larger sense, the term Social Timing could be used to describe the overall social Environment in which the Parent/Child interaction occurs. For example, the Timing of a Parent/Child Relationship during the social conditions of the Ming Dynasty would be a different Environment to the timing of a Parent/Child Relationship during the 50s or 80s in America.

Parent/Child Structure

Parents have the most important and influential role in How Relationships Work. Every culture on Earth upholds and honors child rearing as an activity which requires close attention and supervision. Parents are given the ultimate responsibility in society, creating and training a new human life. The bond initiated between parents and child during the first three years is very strong. The warmer and more nurturing the relationship between parents and child, the more emotionally happy the child will be. By being the first to provide needs for the child, parents establish a precedent for the child in every other relationship.

We are all the creation of two humans who came before us. Their creation of our existence includes our very lives and every way we express it. As such, the primal roles can be given two titles generically speaking. The generic parent role is further divided into the generic mother and generic father roles. These roles are separated by a biological divide. Both roles are required for biological creation to occur.

The Generic Mother Role

Biologically, the Mother provides the egg. Another factor of biology is a nine month period during which the female is carrying the new baby. Assuming the birth goes well for both mother and child, and this is certainly not always the case, the generic mother role would become as follows.

The mother role is the day-to-day caretaker. She manages the minute-to-minute care of the infant. She, dresses and undresses it, bathes, diapers it, feeds it, keeps it warm, puts it to sleep, comforts it, talks to it, and, in general, attends to its every need. The mother is biologically predisposed and socialized to be more emotionally supportive, affectionate, and protective. An infant separated from its mother is susceptible to predators.

Mothers perform the constant maintenance activities, such as bathing, feeding, and cutting the child's hair. They are more likely to do two things at once, such as cooking and talking to their child or speaking on the phone while rocking the cradle.

The Generic Father Role

Biologically, the Father provides the sperm to fertilize the egg. After impregnation he is not needed biologically speaking however if allowed he becomes part of outer parenting along the following lines.

The father role is responsible for supporting the family unit and dealing with the world outside the home. He establishes a relationship with the child through playful interaction. The father is generally stricter, more authoritarian and more aggressive. The influence of his role is said to have more effect-on worldly success and academic achievement. Fathers tend to do the fun, less frequent activities with kids, such as going to the zoo. While they are less likely to do the daily chores, such as preparing breakfast or dinner, they are more likely to perform maintenance chores such as changing oil in the car or mowing the lawn.

Our Experience of Outer Parenting Also Creates Our Initial Self-Parenting Style

Another aspect of these outer roles is their unique contribution to the two internal roles that we create in what I've termed the Inner Parent/Inner Child relationship. As a single child with two parents, we internalize both sides of the outer parenting we received as our "Inner Parent." Our Left Brain records these experiences like a DVD recording so that they can be used as the basis of our Inner Parent.

Our right brain retains and remains our consistent experience of who we are as an "Inner Child." Therefore, our internal Self-Parenting Style begins based on the default template created by the style of the outer parenting we received.

Once you become aware of your inner conversations a person can learn skills to improve his/her default Self-Parenting style. You can learn more about this relationship from my book entitled SELF-PARENTING: The Complete Guide to Your Inner Child.

Suffice to say that the positive skills of Self-Parenting closely resemble the positive skills of outer parenting skills detailed in this chapter.

❹ ROLES

The role of the parent is to love, support, and nurture the child physically, emotionally, mentally, and socially. Parents do this through giving guidance, setting example, and providing a home atmosphere of positive comfort for the child. Another aspect inherent in the Parent Role is how it evolves. In the beginning, parents are the all-encompassing caretakers. The parental role changes as the child matures through several stages.

Parent Role (Generic)

Parent Roles • Physical

The physical role of the parent is to:

- Provide the child's needs for "everyday care"
- Feed and change the child
- Keep the child warm and protected
- Furnish and monitor health care for the child
- Spend time interacting with the child
- Give the child time and attention
- Play with the child
- Give the child abundant hugs and kisses

Parent Roles • Emotional

The emotional role of the parent is to:

- Demonstrate affection for the child
- Demonstrate emotional support for the child
- Talk to and listen to the child
- Comfort the child
- Not be overly possessive of the child
- Keep confidences the child shares with him/her
- Respect the child's need for privacy

- Share important events in the child's life such as birthdays, graduations, and sporting events

Parent Roles • Mental

The mental role of the parent is to:

- Teach and guide the child according to his/her age appropriate role
- Stimulate and encourage the mental development of the child
- Allow the child to pursue his/her own interests
- Respond to or answer questions the child asks
- Monitor the television viewing habits of the child
- Respect the child's own views
- Stimulate and encourage the child to pursue hobbies
- Guide, teach, and encourage good study habits
- Model and teach positive communication methods to the child
- Not force the child to like something against his/her will
- Allow the child to solve his/her own problems

Parent Roles • Social

The social role of the parent is to:

- Enact, teach, and model positive social behavior for the child
- Defend the child against criticism in his/her absence
- Teach and model a positive social example to the child
- Discuss sex and death with the child
- Discuss religion and politics with the child
- Allow the child age appropriate social freedoms
- Encourage age appropriate independence in the child
- Not be critical of the child's choice of friends
- Not have unrealistic expectations of the child

Child Role

The human child has a longer period of parental dependency than any other mammal. The role of the generic child evolves through six age-specific growth stages. For purposes of generalization, each stage will be placed into the corresponding section most closely approximating the physical, emotional, mental, and social roles.

Child Roles • Physical

Newborn (0-1)

The newborn child's role is to have needs and to get them met by mother. During the first year, the newborn's role is passive. It relies completely on the mother for its needs to be met and does not see itself as separate from the mother. The newborn must learn to adapt to a completely new environment. Its role is to learn how to breathe, eat, drink, digest, excrete, stay warm, and cope with stimuli entirely different from the mother's womb.

Child Roles • Emotional

Toddler (1-3)

The toddler's role is to develop its own sense of identity. The toddler is still dependent on its mother for its needs to be met yet it is beginning to assert its own independence. The toddler is also becoming aware of strong feelings which it doesn't understand. As a result, the toddler role is subject to contradictory behaviors of dependence/independence.

Child Roles • Mental

Preschool (3-6)

The preschool child's role is to develop into a little person who is starting to understand and use communication. With the raging inconsistencies of toddlerhood over, the preschooler's role is to explore a new and exciting world.

School Age (6-12)

The school-aged child's role is to learn academic and social skills and to begin socialization within the accepted traditions and customs of the society in which he/she is living.

Child Roles • Social

Adolescence (12-18)

The adolescent child enters a period of intense interaction with peers. The peer group and the child's role within that group becomes the dominant force which further establishes the child's personality as an independent human being. Emulation of others besides family becomes the preferred tactic of the child.

Young Adult (18-25)

Physiologically, the adult child is becoming fully developed and is now expected by society to assume more responsibility for its life. This is the last stage prior to adulthood. The young adult's role is to make major life decisions which will influence his/her growth and direction as a functioning adult within society.

❺ RULES

Parent Rules

Rules for the generic parent are the guidelines for loving, supporting, and nurturing the child.

Parent Rules • Physical

The physical rules of the parent are to:

- Feed the child
- Keep the child warm and protected
- Provide the child's needs for "everyday" care
- Give the child time and attention
- Play with the child
- Furnish and monitor health care for the child

- Give the child abundant hugs and kisses
- Not engage in sexual activity with the child

Parent Rules • Emotional

The emotional rules of the parent are to:

- Demonstrate affection for the child
- Demonstrate emotional support for the child
- Talk to and listen to the child
- Comfort the child
- Not be overly possessive of the child
- Keep the confidences the child shares with them
- Respect the child's need for privacy
- Share important events in the child's life such as birthdays, graduations, and sporting events
- Never tell the child he/she is not as bright or good-looking as they wanted

Parent Rules • Mental

The mental rules of the parent are to:

- Teach and guide the child according to his/her age appropriate role
- Stimulate and encourage the mental development of the child
- Allow the child to pursue his/her own interests
- Respond to or answer questions the child asks
- Monitor the television viewing habits of the child
- Respect the child's own views
- Stimulate and encourage the child to pursue hobbies
- Guide, teach, and encourage good study habits
- Model and teach positive communication methods to the child
- Not force the child to like something against his/her will
- Allow the child to solve his/her own problems

Parent Rules • Social

The social rules of the parent are to:

- Enact, teach, and model positive social interactions with others
- Defend the child against criticism in his/her absence
- Teach and model a positive social behavior for the child example to the child
- Discuss sex and death with the child
- Discuss religion and politics with the child
- Allow the child age appropriate social freedoms
- Encourage age appropriate independence in the child
- Not be critical of the child's choice of friends
- Not have unrealistic expectations of the child

Additional Social Rules for Father

- Stay home with the children when your wife is ill
- Attend children's activities

Child Rules

Rules for the generic child are stage specific, in that there is a different influence and influx of rules at each stage. The child is growing and learning to take its place in society.

Rules for the generic child are to be creative, expressive, respectful, and loving to the Parent. This is accomplished through the process of growing up through the six development stages, each of which has different rules or aspects. Of course, a young child is not consciously aware of following rules; he or she is only doing what comes naturally.

Child Rules • Physical

Baby (0-1) should:

- Breathe, eat, drink, digest, excrete, stay warm, and learn to cope with new stimuli

- Develop his/her body through growth and movement
- Rely completely on the mother or caretaker for survival needs to be met

Child Rules • Emotional

Toddler (1-3) should:

- Begin developing his/her own sense of identity
- Learn to integrate and adapt to the family structure
- Learn to manage daily care activities as they become physiologically able

Child Rules • Mental

Preschool (3-6) should:

- Begin learning and practicing formal communication
- Begin learning the survival rules of society
- Assume chores and tasks as directed by the parents

School Age (6-12) should:

- Learn academic and social skills
- Begin socialization within the accepted traditional customs and usages of the society in which they were born

Child Rules • Social

Adolescence (12-18) should:

- Continue to learn the survival rules of society
- Have increasing family responsibilities as directed by the parents
- Begin an intense period of interaction with peers
- Begin emulation of others besides family as a means of continued development of a sense of independence
- Begin formulating their own ideas and areas of interests

Young Adult (18-25) should:

- Assume adult responsibility for their lives

- Begin making major life decisions that will influence their growth and direction
- Adhere to positive family values and responsibilities
- Begin planning to establish their own living arrangements

❻ CUSTOMS

Parent Customs

Customs in the Parent/Child Relationship depend on the cultural, religious, and political preferences of the parents. Since every sub-group of human society has its own cultural, religious, and political styles, this section is here just to remind you of these categories with some notes.

Parent/Child Customs • Cultural

Cultural birthday traditions are starting to cross-over as people from different cultures interact. In China the first birthday is most auspicious and noodles must be served. The 16th birthday in Barbados is a big affair.

One example of a wide-spread custom in western culture is dressing girls in pink and boys in blue.

Parent/Child Customs • Religious

-
-

Parent/Child Customs • Political

-
-

Parent/Child Co-partners

Here we define the specific personality traits which are most important when playing the Parent (Mother/Father) and Child Roles.

❼ TRAITS

Parent Traits

The traits of the generic parent can be divided into the mother and father roles. Listed here are some of the classic generic traits associated with the male/female participants of the Parent/Child Relationship. Traits by their very nature can be positive or negative.

Positive traits would emphasize the loving, supporting, and nurturing qualities associated with parenting. Negative Traits would call attention to such qualities as abuse and/or neglect.

Parent Traits • Being Attracted

Mother:

There is no deeper sense of being attracted or connected than that shared between mother and child. The mother has carried her child within her for nine months, and nature ensures this bond is continued through the first year of childhood. The mother is biologically programmed to love and want to be with her child, and the child is biologically unable to survive without the close physical attention provided by the mother or mother substitute.

Father:

The father is less biologically connected than the mother but he, too, can feel attracted to his child during the early years. Although the early parental support generally comes from the mother, during school age and adolescence the father becomes more prominent as a role model and disciplinary figure. This connection to the father is an important requirement for the psychological health of the child.

Parent Traits • Being Committed

Being Committed is the essential trait of the Parent/Child Relationship. Ideally, both parents will be committed to raising and nurturing their child through the six stages.

Mother:

The generic, mother is more biologically and emotionally committed to parenting. She has a predisposed ability to bond with the child. She feels a great responsibility and desire to love, nurture, and protect her child.

Father:

The generic father is more able to waive commitment on a biological basis. Yet the Father may be as committed as the mother or more so according to the parenting Traits of the individual father.

Parent Traits • Being Genuine

There is no possible way for either parent to fake the trait of being genuine with their children. The proximity and intimacy Parent/Child Relationship is simply too strong. Plus, the intuitive nature of the child is too perceptive.

Mother:

The mother, as the primary caretaker, is most likely to experience and express genuine feelings of love, support, and nurture for the child.

Father:

The Father as the secondary caretaker, is more likely to be outside the Parent/Child intimacy asked of the relationship. Matters such as financial responsibilities and social interaction give the father more opportunity to mask, hide, or avoid his true genuine self.

Parent Traits • Being Trustworthy

Being Trustworthy is more noticeable in its absence than presence in the Parent/Child Relationship. Ideally, parents would be utterly trustworthy and dependable when concerned with all family affairs, not just Parent/Child dynamics.

In the world of human nature, however, there is ample room for mother, father, or both to be untrustworthy in relating to their children. If this is the case, the Parent/Child Relationship suffers in a terrible way. Many times, this is the result of stresses occurring outside the Parent/Child Relationship itself, such as financial or job stress, marital difficulties, chemical dependencies, parental illness/death, or other outside factors which impair the trustworthiness quotient of the parent.

Parent Traits • Being Emotionally Mature

Emotional Maturity is vital to successful parenting by the generic parent. Adolescents and Young Adults are able to have children physically before they have matured emotionally. In this situation, it is imperative that there be strong family support to take care of the needs of the child.

Mother:

Maturity for the mother represents her ability to give her child the full attention he or she deserves despite the sacrifice and commitment required. The immature mother may be unable or unwilling to give her child full attention due to the insufficiency of her own biological or emotional development.

Father:

Maturity for the father role represents his ability and willingness to provide for the family's welfare by working and supporting the wife in her primary role as mother.

Parent Traits • Having Communication Skills

Communication skills are a trait highly valued in the parent. A child is naturally predisposed to value and hold in high regard anything the parent says. If the parents can be clear and direct in their communication, the child will be able to understand almost intuitively.

It is also important to remember that parents are always communicating their thoughts and feelings to their child whether the parents realize it or not. Everything the parents say and do is being communicated to and absorbed as gospel by their children.

Parent Traits • Having Problem-Solving

Problem-solving skills are constantly required by both parents in the Parent/Child Relationship. Without the ability of the parents to initiate this essential human function, the Parent/Child Relationship will be a negative experience for everyone concerned. A strong commitment to positive problem-solving by both parents is necessary for the Parent/Child Relationship to function smoothly.

Initiating problem-solving is the responsibility of the parental role. Even when the child is still an infant, the parents can begin to initiate problem-solving skills non-verbally. As the child matures the parents must model and teach their child how to participate in the Win/Win solutions required for true problem-solving. It is inappropriate for the child to need to initiate this skill in the Parent/Child relationship.

Child Traits

Other than traits 5, 6, and 7, a child is naturally disposed toward positive Traits. As a result of being a child, he or she will he attracted, committed, genuine, and trustworthy in an age appropriate manner. Yet, based on the type of parenting a child receives, he/she can have his/her natural traits altered or transformed.

Child Traits • Being Attracted

The child is entirely attracted and connected to his/her parents especially from the infant to adolescence stage. The child relies entirely on the good will of his/her parents for love, support, and nurturing and does not know any other reality.

Child Traits • Being Committed

A child is committed to the Parent/Child Relationship unless the relationship becomes a source of pain which the child must then reject. Even so, before ten, it is impossible for a child not to be committed (bonded) to the parent. This is because the Parent/Child Relationship is the natural source of its existence and well-being.

Child Traits • Being Genuine

A child is naturally genuine unless he/she learns or is taught how not to be.

Child Traits • Being Trustworthy

A child is naturally trustworthy unless he/she is taught otherwise. At certain ages, it may be a part of the child's learning experience to lie or steal things, but this is simply experimental behavior. It's a part of the child's learning and socialization process.

Of course, a young child should not be expected to be trustworthy at adult levels until he/she has matured physically, emotionally, and mentally enough to fully understand what is meant by trustworthiness. If outside problems affect the trustworthiness of the parents (i.e. drug addiction problems), the child will simply be unable to trust due to the particular conditions or state of its parents.

Child Traits • Being Emotionally Mature

Emotional maturity is one trait not expected of the child until he/she approaches Adolescence and Young Adult stage. Even then, the mistakes a child makes through immaturity are part of the learning experiences needed to establish and deepen the trait of emotional maturity.

Child Traits • Having Communication Skills

Children first learn to communicate by copycatting the communication style of their parents. Next, they learn the traditional skills of society's communication methods throughout their school years.

Child Traits • Having Problem-Solving Skills

Although willing to problem-solve, children are unable to initiate this behavior because of their unskilled and relative powerlessness in the Parent/Child Relationship.

Children learn to problem-solve by watching family interactions or by being a happy participant in the process as initiated by their parents and or teachers.

Once a child learns how to problem-solve, he/she is usually very willing to solve conflicts in a Win/Win way. If a positive model for problem-solving is not provided by the parents, the child will have a more difficult time learning or trusting this skill outside the family.

❽ NEEDS

Parent Needs

The Needs of the generic parent closely follow the generic roles of the relationship as outlined in the relationship Structure. One thing that parents must be careful of is to not attempt using the Parent/Child Structure to meet needs that it was not designed to fulfill.

For example, a parent may attempt to make up for a lack of personal self-esteem by using the child's love as a substitute. A mother may try to compensate for the lack of love in a marriage relationship by spoiling her child. Or, a father may attempt to make a child become, the athlete he never was. Unfortunately, self-love or true self-esteem cannot be supplied in this way.

Parent Needs • Physical

Parents need to physically provide for the child. This includes the caretaking and support functions. Although this need isn't as apparent, as the parent's age, they will necessarily have a physical need to be taken care of by their children. By providing for their children now, there is an implied expectation to have their physical needs met when they are older and become Aging Parents.

Parent Needs • Emotional

Parents need to love, nurture, and support their child. They want to flow the love they feel inside of them to their children. When they give love to their child they feel this love within themselves. And when the child returns this love and attention, the parents feel warmed emotionally.

Parent Needs • Mental

Parents need to teach their child. They want their child to grow and mature with the background and training needed to succeed in life. This passing on of their intellectual knowledge and strengths is rewarding. Every Parent wants their Child to avoid the mistakes that he/she made.

Parent Needs • Social

Parents need to see the child successfully integrated into society. They want their child to "succeed" as a reflection or an extension of their success as parents. If their child is successful socially, this enhances their social status.

Child Needs

The generic child needs to bond with his/her parents and to feel a part of the family. This is how the child learns and grows. Bonding occurs during the first three to seven years of life.

If the parent has been a positive influence for the child, the child will be well prepared for his/her assimilation into society. If the parent has not fulfilled the positive model of parenting, the child will attain social success only by battling against immense odds.

Child Needs • Physical

A child must meet his/her physical and survival needs as well as feel a sense of security and safety.

Child Needs • Emotional

A child needs to feel loved, supported, and valued as part of the family unit and be free to love others and express itself emotionally.

Child Needs • Mental

More growth and learning occur in a child from birth to age seven than will occur in the rest of his/her lifetime. During this most intimate period, parents have an all-powerful influence on the Child's growth and learning which impacts him/her forever.

The child is constantly observing and absorbing information from his/her environment and structuring this information into a basis for future operating in the world. The child will later turn this information, along with his/her natural curiosity and interests, into lifelong passions and pursuits.

Child Needs • Social

A child needs to be accepted and included in whatever social environment he or she is in. As this yearning develops through the six childhood stages, the child will have countless experiences of socialization.

From the complete range of options the child will navigate a unique course on the way to expressing his/her personality individually and collectively within the culture he/she is born and lives.

❾ TACTICS

Parent Tactics

Positive Tactics that best ensure success are those that develop and use the skills of positive parenting. By pursuing these Tactics, parents can make many positive contributions to the Parent/Child Relationship.

Parent Tactics • Positive

Positive Tactics for the Parent are:

- Talking lovingly to the child when he/she is young
- Reading to the child
- Staying home with the child when he/she is sick
- Spending physical time with the child
- Monitoring the television watching of your child (Third graders spend an average of 900 hours a year in class and 1170 hours watching television.)
- Appreciate your child for his/her good points

Parent Tactics •Negative

Negative Tactics for the Parent are:

- Yelling and screaming at the child
- Relying excessively on television as a baby sitter
- Using bribes to gain the child's good behavior
- Telling personal "war stories" when you were never in a war

Child Tactics

The child's Tactics are to explore the new environment in which he/she lives. Children will attempt to do anything they can get away with. For example, the Tactics of an infant are to put everything it can get its hands on into its mouth.

A child's Tactics in the Parent/Child Relationship are particularly stage-sensitive. The child will employ differing Tactics as it matures. It learns and develops by playing strategies against the foundation of the family rules. Later, these strategies become the child's foundation for following society's rules.

Child Tactics • Positive

Some positive Tactics for a child are:

- Telling the truth
- Not taking without asking
- Asking permission from both parents

Child Tactics • Negative

Some negative Tactics for a child are:

- Lying
- Taking without asking
- Playing mom against dad for favors

CHAPTER 8

*T*he Sibling/Sibling Relationship

Sibling/Sibling Relationships have the distinction of being the longest-lasting human relationships. They are also the second-strongest kinship bond, following the Parent/Child Relationship. The Sibling/Sibling Relationship begins with the birth of your brothers and/or sisters, and you.

Siblings are the family members that establish and fill out the basic unit of society, the Family. Siblings develop extremely close ties through such activities as walking or traveling to school together and going on family trips, especially when the siblings are close in age.

Siblings can also bond closely in adult life which takes on the additional characteristics of the Friend/Friend Relationship. When siblings have grown into adulthood, their mutual activities include:

- Interacting with each other
- Providing assistance to other family members
- Keeping up with the family news
- Attending holiday celebrations or anniversaries
- They often live with each other

Sibling/Sibling Environment

❶ LOCATION

The physical Location of a Sibling/Sibling Environment is the family home with the inclusion of either a brother(s) and/or a sister(s). Some important factors of the Sibling/ Sibling Location are:

- The quality of the relationship between the parents
- The neighborhood in which they live
- The family's socio-economic status

Siblings are involved with intimate contact in the home Location every day. They share genetic and environmental characteristics as well as the family name. They may share a bedroom or possibly even a bed. Siblings usually continue to share their relationship environment throughout adolescence.

❷ DURATION

As mentioned previously, the Sibling/Sibling Relationship is typically the human relationship with the longest lasting duration. This is because the two Co-partners enter the relationship early in life and remain siblings biologically speaking for life.

❸ TIMING

The primary Timing of the Sibling/Sibling Relationship takes place when siblings are living with their parents. Researchers are currently defining the generic traits and attributes associated with each sibling according to birth order.

Historic Timing of the Sibling/Sibling Environment refers to the social conditions of the society in which the family lives. For example, family life as a sibling in New York City during the 1790s would have different Historic Timing than family life in NYC during the 1990s.

Sibling/Sibling Structure

In many ways, the Structure of the Sibling/Sibling Relationship may be the most neglected because it is so close to the Co-partners that they don't question it. This can be a good news/bad news situation. The good news is that problems with this structure aren't the major thing people complain about. The bad news is that when a problem does develop, there are not a lot of guidelines for how to proceed.

The Sibling/Sibling Relationship has three sub-categories of sibling roles. They are:

- Sister to Sister
- Brother to Sister
- Brother to Brother

Sister to Sister Roles

The bond between sisters is the strongest. Adult sisters keep in closest touch and have the most in common. Women in the family are known as the kin keepers.

Brother to Sister Roles

Different alliances may be established depending on birth order of the siblings.

Brother to Brother Roles

The bond between brothers is the weakest of the three Roles. However that's not to say that the Brother/Brother Relationship couldn't be deep and meaningful for certain siblings depending on the Co-partners and family dynamics.

❹ ROLES

The Role of the generic Sibling is to support and protect each other. Practicing these skills establishes a foundation for helping and serving others outside the family.

Sibling Role • Physical

Physically, the Role of a Sibling is to:

- Protect each other from physical or environmental stress and danger
- Watch out for each other's safety
- Share food, water, and shelter, particularly in stressful or dangerous situations
- Respect the privacy needs of each other

Sibling Role • Emotional

Emotionally, the Role of a Sibling is to:

- Keep in touch
- Provide help when needed or if asked
- Show emotional support
- Address each other by first name
- Give birthday cards and holiday presents
- Not be jealous of each other
- Keep confidences
- Share news of success
- Not be overprotective each other
- Treat each other as friends
- Ask for personal advice if appropriate

Sibling Role • Mental

Mentally, the Role of a Sibling is to:

- Advise each other
- Listen to each other's advice
- Help each other meet their mental needs
- Teach each other
- Learn from each other

Sibling Role • Social

Socially, the Role of a Sibling is to:

- Be supportive in matters outside the family
- Visit, help, and offer congratulations when a new child is born to another sibling
- Not interfere in each other's social relationships
- Defend each other against criticism when the other is absent
- Help each other get along with their friends
- Not criticize each other publicly
- Attend family gatherings

❺ RULES

The Rules of the Sibling/Sibling Relationships closely follow their role responsibilities.

Sibling Rules • Physical

Physically, the Rules of a Sibling are to:

- Protect each other from physical or environmental stress and danger
- Watch out for each other's safety
- Share food, water, and shelter, particularly in stressful or dangerous situations
- Respect the privacy needs of each other

Sibling Rules • Emotional

Emotionally, the Rules of a Sibling are to:

- Keep in touch
- Provide help when needed or if asked
- Show emotional support
- Address each other by first name
- Give birthday cards and holiday presents
- Not be jealous of each other
- Keep confidences
- Share news of success
- Not be overprotective

- Treat each other as friends
- Ask for personal advice if appropriate

Sibling Rules • Mental

Mentally, the Rules of a Sibling are to:

- Advise each other
- Listen to each other's advice
- Help each other meet their mental needs
- Teach each other
- Learn from each other

Sibling Rules • Social

Socially, the Rules of a Sibling are to:

- Be supportive in matters outside the family
- Visit, help, and offer congratulations when a new child is born to another sibling
- Not interfere in each other's social relationships
- Defend each other against criticism when the other is absent
- Help each other get along with their friends
- Not criticize each other publicly
- Attend family gatherings

➏ CUSTOMS

Sibling Customs • Cultural

It is natural for siblings of all cultures to tease, torment, and torture each other.

Sibling Customs • Religious

Sibling Customs • Political

Hire your brother to be attorney general.

Sibling/Sibling Co-partners

Evaluating the Two Co-partners in a Sibling/Sibling Relationship is interesting since there can be such a variety of personalities playing the sibling role, even though the siblings have the same parents and share the same Environment.

❼ TRAITS

Since Siblings are connected by birth and remain involved in a longest intimate relationship, the positive or negative Traits of each sibling become a pivotal factor in their relationship.

Sibling Traits • Being Attracted

Siblings are more than attracted through kinship; they are connected. Attraction become a practical matter in deciding how much time Siblings want to spend together once they have moved out of the family environment. If you like your sibling, you will see each other more often. If siblings live in close proximity, they often socialize, especially if they are close in age. They are especially likely to see each other at family gatherings, such as holidays and birthdays.

Sibling Traits • Being Committed

Commitment in the Sibling/Sibling Relationship is built-in. Many people spend an inordinate amount of time trying to help siblings when they would never do the same for a stranger.

Although a sibling's personal traits may be so bad he/she would be written off by anyone else, family members will tend to overlook them in the name of familial loyalty and obligation.

Sibling Traits • Being Genuine

Siblings would ideally be genuine with each other. Part of the relationship is that if you try to "put one over" on a sibling, he or she will see right through you. During adolescence, when peer group interactions become more important than family, siblings may practice their new personalities on each other.

Other conditions, such as alcohol or drug addiction, can cause a Sibling to make dramatic trait reversals from established family patterns. A good example here is the crack-addicted brother in Spike Lee's movie, "Jungle Fever."

Sibling Traits • Being Trustworthy

Being trustworthy should be an absolute given in the Sibling/Sibling Relationship, but special care should be taken not to let family duty overrule if the traits of a sibling definitely prove untrustworthy.

For example, a sibling may never gain maturity in handling money matters. Or a sibling might be forever being bailed out of minor or major scrapes by family members.

Sibling Traits • Being Emotionally Mature

Being Emotionally Mature is another trait that family members seem to overlook or forgive quite easily. When growing up, all the siblings are immature. Perhaps if a sibling has been behaving in an immature manner all his/her life, the fact that he or she is now 42 years old doesn't really "click in."

Sibling Traits • Having Communication Skills

Ideally, positive communication skills will be absorbed naturally through the example of positive communication within the family unit.

Siblings learn their style of expressing needs and interacting with others through the constant interaction of family members. Even when a sibling has developed positive communication skills in other areas of social and business, he or she quite often reverts to the old patterns when communicating with siblings.

Sibling Traits • Having Problem-Solving Skills

Problem-solving will first be practiced as siblings when a myriad of daily situations require the willingness to resolve conflict, to share, and to take turns. If healthy patterns are established as children, then as adults the Siblings should have positive interactions.

❽ NEEDS

As the Co-partners in the Sibling/Sibling Relationship get older, their needs become more like a Friend/Friend Relationship. They keep the same needs, but their motivations to see each other becomes more like that of a friend. In fact, really good friends are sometimes given the honorary status as siblings when you see them all the time and they are like part of the family. The following are the needs as reflected when the Siblings are living as a family.

Sibling Needs • Physical

Physically, the Needs of a Sibling are:

- Protect each other from physical or environmental stress and danger
- Watch out for each other's safety
- Share food, water, and shelter, particularly in stressful or dangerous situations
- Respect the privacy needs of each other
- Not to have too many "borrowing the clothes" problems

Sibling Needs • Emotional

Emotionally, the Needs of a Sibling are to:

- Keep in touch
- Provide help when needed or if asked
- Show emotional support
- Address each other by first name
- Give birthday cards and holiday presents
- Not be jealous of each other
- Keep confidences
- Share news of success
- Not be overprotective

- Treat each other as friends
- Ask for personal advice if appropriate

Sibling Needs • Mental

Mentally, the Needs of a Sibling are

- Advise each other
- Listen to each other's advice
- Help each other to meet their mental needs
- Teach each other
- Learn from each other

Sibling Needs • Social

Socially, the Needs of a Sibling are to:

- Be supportive in matters outside the family
- Visit, help, and offer congratulations when a new child is born to another sibling
- Not interfere in each other's social relationships
- Defend each other against criticism when the other is absent
- Help each other get along with their friends
- Not criticize each other publicly
- Attend family gatherings

❾ TACTICS

Sibling Tactics • Positive

- Following the PEMS Roles and Rules
- Sharing, taking turns
- Being honest when it counts
- Supporting the Sibling through tough times

Sibling Tactics • Negative

- Not following the PEMS Roles and Rules
- Not sharing, taking turns
- Not being honest when it counts
- Not supporting the Sibling through tough times
- Sisters dating other sister's boyfriends
- Brothers dating other brother's girlfriends

Special Note: Birth Order:

Birth order has two special aspects which dramatically impact the dynamics of the Sibling/Sibling Relationship:

- The parents' parenting style becomes successively more lenient as each child is born.
- Each child typically adopts a characteristic pattern of behavior that is consistent with his/her order of appearance in the family.

These patterns effect not only the sibling interactions but the entire dynamics of the family. For example, a first born is treated with an entirely different set of expectations by parents than a fifth born. The second sibling, in order to establish his/her own individuality, often behaves in a manner that is in direct rebellion to the personality of the first born.

As each successive sibling is born, he/she experiences distinctive responses from the family that influences the sibling's relationship to parents, each other, and the world.

The Grandparent/ Grandchild Relationship

The Grandparent/Grandchild Relationship is often the closest relationship outside the immediate family because the children's parents keep in close contact with their own parents.

Grandparents have the potential to help their Grandchildren with treasured support. They can provide the Grandchild with a more relaxed experience of love and sharing simply by holding hands while walking through the park. The Grandchild provides a special gift to his/her Grandparents with the warm happiness in his/her eyes or a big hug. This is the one relationship that has the most potential to build treasured and cherished memories for both Co-partners.

Many of the classic problems of the "Grandparent-as-a-Parent" seem to magically disappear once the Grandchildren start arriving much to the surprise and relief of the "Child-who-has-now-become" a Parent.

Grandparent/Grandchild Environment

❶ LOCATION

The location for the Grandparent/Grandchild Relationship will most likely be the grandparents' home. Grandchildren are often taken to their grandparents' home for vacations, family gatherings, and holiday celebrations. Also, the grandparents may visit the parents' home for extended stays (or the children may visit the grandparents) such as during the summer. Another possibility for the Grandparent/Grandchild environment may be one or more grandparents living permanently with the family.

❷ DURATION

This relationship could be a shorter term relationship than other family relationships because of the age of the grandparents. However, if the Grandparents are young, a Grandchild could possibly be on the seesaw structure with the Grandparents throughout their final years in life. The loss of a beloved Grandparent could be a Grandchild's first personal experience of bereavement.

❸ TIMING

If the parents live close to their parents, the grandparents may see or visit their grandchildren on a regular basis for shared activities such as visiting the zoo or babysitting. As the grandparents age, they might move into the home with parents or into a nursing home.

Grandparent/Grandchild Structure

❹ ROLES

Grandparent Role

Grandparents assume the Role of being head of the clan and usually feel extremely close to their grandchildren. Since they have few disciplinary responsibilities, they simply enjoy the company of the young. Grandparents frequently take the child's side during conflicts between parent and child.

The grandfather is often the family figurehead and may assist family members financially by paying school fees or through eventual inheritance.

The grandmother is especially important to her daughters and their families. She is able to establish a more successful relationship with her granddaughters than the relationship between Grandfathers and Grandsons. This is because of the similarity between generic female roles and interests.

Grandparent Role • Physical

- –
- –

Grandparent Role • Emotional

- –
- –

Grandparent Role • Mental

- –
- –

Grandparent Role • Social

- –
- –

Grandchild Role

Grandchildren enjoy interacting with their grandparents because grandparents are usually eager to spoil them and the grandchildren enjoy the attention.

Grandchild Role • Physical

–

–

Grandchild Role • Emotional

–

–

Grandchild Role • Mental

–

–

Grandchild Role • Social

–

–

❺ RULES

Grandparent Rules

Grandparent Rules • Physical

Physically the Grandparent should:

– Baby sit the grandchild
– Give financial aid and support if possible

Grandparent Rules • Emotional

Emotionally the Grandparent should:

– Shower the grandchild with unconditional love
– Be a positive companion during mutual activities

Grandparent Rules • Mental

Mentally the Grandparent should:

- Pay attention to and support the grandchild
- Take the grandchild on trips and educational excursions

Grandparent Rules • Social

Socially the Grandparent should:

- Respect the child as a clan member
- Make an effort to see each grandchild as a unique individual

Grandchild Rules

Grandchild Rules • Physical

Physically the Grandchild should:

-
-

Grandchild Rules • Emotional

Emotionally the Grandchild should:

-
-

Grandchild Rules • Mental

Mentally the Grandchild should:

-
-

Grandchild Rules • Social

Socially the Grandchild should:

-
-

❻ CUSTOMS

Grandparents are often the closest links to traditional social customs that children will have. This is especially true if the grandparents are from the "old country."

Grandparent/Grandchild Customs • Cultural

‑

‑

‑

Grandparent/Grandchild Customs • Religious

‑

‑

‑

Grandparent/Grandchild Customs • Political

‑

‑

‑

Grandparent/Grandchild Co-partners

❼ TRAITS

Grandparent Traits

Positive Traits of the grandparents become especially important if the parents are unwilling or unable to fulfill their roles as parents. Many times concerned grandparents will take on the physical, emotional, or financial responsibility to raise a grandchild if parents become negligent or if a tragedy occurs and a child loses his/her parents. Grandparents often carry out a critical family function if required to step in and fulfill parental obligations.

Grandparents may also have negative Traits that impact the family. For example, they may be unsociable, abusive, or alcoholic. Since they are trusted members of the family and often have babysitting responsibilities, the grandparents' Traits could often be put to the test.

A grandchild is particularly vulnerable as any complaints or observations about the parent's parents are likely to go unheeded or create extremely volatile emotional issues.

Grandparent Traits • Being Attracted

Under normal circumstances, the grandparents will certainly be attracted to their grandchild. Grandchildren provide the grandparents with certified continuance of their family line. They are usually more than willing to take care of the grandchild in any way that is manageable by them. As the grandchild grows, the grandparents typically enjoy being a companion for the grandchild.

Grandparent Traits • Being Committed

Ideally, grandparents will be committed to supporting and nurturing the grandchild. The circumstances of where everyone lives and how much money everyone has will be an important factor. Because the grandparents have already gone the distance with their children, they view their grandchild as a bonus. Also, a grandchild brings new experiences along with fresh energy and purpose to the classic family interactions.

Grandparent Traits • Being Genuine

Being genuine is not the most important Trait in the Grandparent/Grandchild Relationship. The interaction of the relationship is not based on each Co-partner communicating their true thoughts and feelings. Perhaps the grandparents might even use the opportunity of a captive audience to retell many of the family stories stressing their particular version of events.

Grandparent Traits • Being Trustworthy

Being Trustworthy is an important Trait if the grandparents are given any authority or responsibility for the grandchild. This includes not only the relationship between the grandparent and grandchild but the general trustworthiness of the responsible grandparent. Will he/she forget to fasten the grandchild's safety belt? Will he/she leave the grandchild unattended to go have a drink?

Grandparent Traits • Being Emotionally Mature

The grandparents will usually have enough emotional maturity to play their part in the Grandparent/Grandchild Relationship. Again, this Trait is not as crucial a part of the relationship interaction. However, a grandparent's emotional maturity in relating to the parents regarding the grandchildren could be an issue.

Grandparent Traits • Having Communications Skills

Communications skills would be an appropriate trait for the grandparents to demonstrate. The general communication style of the parents will often match the grandparents anyhow. Since grandparents often have more time to spend with a grandchild, they would enjoy having conversations and sharing ideas with the grandchild.

Grandparent Traits • Having Problem-Solving Skills

Problems will develop in any relationship, even one between grandparents and grandchild. Grandparents can often be put in the role of problem-solving due to their status in the family hierarchy. If they are good at solving problem this Trait will come in handy in a variety of potential circumstances. Just becoming aware of a grandchild's problems would be a good first step.

Grandchild Traits

Grandchild Traits • Being Attracted

The grandchild is naturally willing be with the grandparents. They have usually been introduced to their grandparents early and feel comfortable around them. They have an intuitive understanding and respect for the grandparents as the source of who they are.

Grandchild Traits • Being Committed

The grandchild is usually the effect of the circumstances surrounding the Parent/Child interaction. In this sense, the grandchild is typically willing to go along with what it's asked to do. As the grandchild enters school age and adolescence, he/she may have a special relationship with a grandparent in which they interact quite often. Or, they may reject spending time with the grandparents in lieu of spending more time with their peers.

Grandchild Traits • Being Genuine

A grandchild is likely to be very genuine with a grandparent until such time as its personal social needs begin to conflict with the needs of a member from the "older generation."

Grandchild Traits • Being Trustworthy

A grandchild is likely to be trustworthy from his/her side of the relationship unless it has taught not to be or has had his/her trust violated in some way by the grandparents.

Grandchild Traits • Being Emotionally Mature

A grandchild would not typically be expected or required to be emotionally mature in the Grandparent/Grandchild Relationship.

Grandchild Traits • Having Communications Skills

The expression and communication of the grandchild in the relationship will be determined by the age and emotional maturity of the grandchild.

Grandchild Traits • Having Problem-Solving Skills

Problem-solving skills would not be a Trait that is the responsibility of a grandchild.

❽ NEEDS

Grandparent Needs

Grandparent Needs • Physical

- To feel a sense of biological continuity
- To want to protect and nurture kin

Grandparent Needs • Emotional

- To feel satisfaction from passing on traditions
- To indulge and show leniency towards the grandchild
- To share and be with the grandchildren
- To experience emotional self-fulfillment through the grandchild

Grandparent Needs • Mental

- To be respected as the family patriarch/matriarch
- To pass on wisdom and knowledge to the "younger generation"
- To learn and experience joy through the eyes of a grandchild

Grandparent Needs • Social

- The concept of grandparenthood is often central to their lives in the same way that parenthood is to parents
- Bragging about the grandchildren is a requirement of old age
- To share and preserve memories of the clan with other clan members

Grandchild Needs

A grandchild's needs are met because they have another source of fulfillment similar to their parents but with more stress-free and possibly adventuresome aspects. They are more likely to be spoiled and obtain advantages that are impossible to receive from their parents.

Grandchild Needs • Physical

- To have a mature companion to be taken care of by
- To be supervised by a responsible adult in physical activities such as running and playing in the park

Grandchild Needs • Emotional

- Someone to listen to them
- Someone to pay attention to them
- Someone to care about who they are in a personal way

Grandchild Needs • Mental

- Someone to teach them and take them for educational outings
- The desire to learn and explore new environments

Grandchild Needs • Social

- To feel part of a social clan
- To attend family gatherings
- To interact with other family members at birthdays, holiday celebrations and family events such as weddings

❾ TACTICS

Grandparent Tactics

Grandparent Tactics • Positive

Some examples of positive Tactics of the grandparent are:

- Grandparents often take the side of the grandchild during Parent/Child disputes.
- Spoiling the grandchild (in a nice way) is a major tactic of most grandparents.

Grandparent Tactics • Negative

Some examples of negative Tactics of the grandparent are:

- If the grandmother is cold, she will put a sweater on her grandchild
- A Grandparent might "buy" the grandchild's love with material possessions as a form of manipulation to "win love"
- Giving a Grandchild large sums of money to present themselves as superior to the Parents or other Grandparents

Grandchild Tactics

Grandchild Tactics • Positive

Some examples of positive tactics of the grandchild are:

- To run and hug the grandparents when they arrive
- To create pictures and gifts for the grandparents
- To excitedly relate their whole day to the rapt grandparent

Grandchild Tactics • Negative

Some examples of negative tactics of the grandchild could be:

- To run and hide when the grandparents arrive
- To keep watching TV as opposed to greeting or speaking with the Grandparent

CHAPTER 10

*T*he Kin/Kin Relationships

Kinship is an important role for humans. In western society, the main kinship attachments occur within the immediate family of siblings and grandparents. The frequency of contact between aunts, uncles, cousins, nephews, and nieces is much less than for primary kin. There are fewer obligations to keep in touch by phone or letter than between parents and siblings. Social contacts usually occur through reunions held by the parents (who are siblings).

Third world cultures have much larger groups of extended kin. Many cultures have extended families of 300 or more members who remain in constant contact.

Kin/Kin Environment

❶ LOCATION

The Location, their proximity to you, where each relative lives, is probably going to affect your relationship more than any other factor. If certain relatives live far away, the likelihood of seeing them often diminishes proportionately. The types of opportunities you have to see each other will create the physical location of your interaction. For example, you will interact with your Aunts and Uncles at family gatherings. Family births, deaths, and anniversaries will be observed at a location dictated by your customs.

Depending on your age, you may interact with your cousins during these same types of family events or go out to social functions one-on-one. As you get older you will probably have more choice in your opportunities to see nephews and nieces at holiday celebrations, school graduations, and family get-togethers.

❷ DURATION

Again, the Duration of each of your Kin/Kin Relationships will depend on how close your relatives live or your schedule for seeing or visiting them during the year. Because there are so many potential Kin/Kin combinations, your Durations could be completely different depending on your age and the type of Kin you have.

❸ TIMING

The Timing of your Kin/Kin Relationship Relationships will vary. You may visit your aunt or uncle for two weeks each summer. You could see your cousin every day at school. You might see a nephew or niece for two hours every Wednesday when you baby sit for your brother or sister. Since there are so many types of Kin/Kin Relationships, there can be many variations as to the Timing of their interactions.

Kin/Kin Structure

❹ ROLES

Aunt/Uncle Role

The role of the Aunt/Uncle is to be a kind, supportive additional family member for the nieces and nephews. This might include babysitting on a regular basis or during family emergencies, or being a supportive family member in other ways.

Sometimes Aunts/Uncles can take the place of parents or act as second parents when looking after the children. Their influence is more prominent when the children are younger. In many cultures the Aunts/Uncles have the same parenting rights and role as the biological parents.

Aunt/Uncle Role • Physical

- Aunts and Uncles are there to help or babysit, especially when the children are younger
- Could take care of you, the family member, if your parents are sick
- Relatives may be a source of financial assistance

Aunt/Uncle Role • Emotional

- Sometimes your might be able to tell your aunt or uncle something that you cannot tell your parents
- They might be able to help you out with problems that the parents might not
- They may be more neutral or not as over-protective
- They may be emotionally supportive when you have nowhere else to go

Aunt/Uncle Role • Mental

- Aunts and Uncles are there to give their point of view on discipline
- You might be able to turn to them for advice

- They may be a sounding board for ideas
- They may be in the position to teach you a trade or new discipline

Aunt/Uncle Role • Social

- Aunts and Uncles can be there to help with functions or parties
- They could take you to the zoo, or a museum
- They are often supportive and part of birthdays, holidays, graduations
- Often provide support with a welcoming attitude or open door policy

Niece/Nephew Role

Niece/Nephew Role • Physical

The role of the nephew or niece is to:

- Be the play toy for the older Aunt/Uncle, according to their age in the family
- Participate in family events

Niece/Nephew Role • Emotional

The role of the nephew or niece is to:

- Be happy in the family environment
- To share
- Have respect for adult kin
- If multicultural may help out with translations or form filling or assist in similar ways

Niece/Nephew Role • Mental

The role of the nephew or niece is to:

- To learn family history and stories
- To draw additional experiences and insights from trusted family sources

Niece/Nephew Role • Social

The role of the nephew or niece is to:

- Attend family get-togethers
- Visit the Aunt/Uncle out of respect
- Give gifts/share birthdays and holidays
- Follow family obligations and rituals

Cousins Role

As a young cousin, you will likely see your other young cousins because of family interactions or proximity in living arrangements. As you approach your later teenage years, you may have more opportunity to socialize with a cousin that lived near by during childhood.

If you have many cousins, you will usually like one or two cousins more than the rest. The one you like best is likely to be the same sex, related through the mother (oftentimes her sister), and to have been a childhood companion.

An ongoing relationship with a cousin is more voluntary than interactions with your closer kin and can assume characteristics similar to Friend/Friend Relationships.

Cousin Role • Physical

Physically, Cousins should:

- Help each other in any way they can
- Protect each other from danger
- Share possessions as might be necessary

Cousin Role • Emotional

Emotionally, Cousins should:

- Talk about family issues
- Try to help each other during family problems
- Be emotionally supportive of kin in crisis

Cousin Role • Mental

Mentally, Cousins should:

- Help the other by giving advice
- Be on the lookout for mutual opportunities

Cousin Role • Social

Socially, Cousins should:

- Attend family get-togethers
- Visit each other as often as practical

❺ RULES

Aunt/Uncle Rules

Aunt/Uncle Rules • Physical

Physically, Aunts/Uncles should:

- Protect their nieces/nephews from danger or harm
- Be willing to babysit or mind their nieces/nephews

Aunt/Uncle Rules • Emotional

Emotionally, Aunts/Uncles should:

- Share time with their nieces/nephews
- Support nieces/nephews through contact and activities

Aunt/Uncle Rules • Mental

Mentally, Aunts/Uncles should:

- Teach their nieces/nephews
- Read to their nieces/nephews

Aunt/Uncle Rules • Social

Socially, Aunts/Uncles should:

- Attend birthday parties for their nieces/nephews
- Support the nieces/nephews during family traumas such as sickness, death, or suicide

Niece/Nephew Rules

Niece/Nephew Rules • Physical

-
-

Niece/Nephew Rules • Emotional

-
-

Niece/Nephew Rules • Mental

-
-

Niece/Nephew Rules • Social

-
-

Cousins Rules

Cousin Rules • Physical

Physically, Cousins should:

- Protect their cousins from danger or harm
- Be willing to hang out with their cousins
- Help each other any way they can
- Be able to rely on each such as borrowing and repaying money

Cousin Rules • Emotional

Emotionally, Cousins should:

- Share time with their Cousins
- Be able to talk about family issues and share problems
- Try to help each other during personal or family problems
- Be good friends and act as siblings

Cousin Rules • Mental

Mentally, Cousins should:

- Teach their Cousins
- Read to their Cousins
- Help each other by giving advice
- Be on the lookout for mutual opportunities

Cousin Rules • Social

Socially, Cousins should:

- Attend family get-togethers such as birthday parties and graduations
- Support each other during family traumas such as sickness, death, or suicide
- Visit each other often
- Protect and defend the family name
- Attend weddings, funerals, etc
- Go out with each other in social non-family adventures
- Strive to keep family secrets
- Strive to keep family support systems healthy

❻ CUSTOMS

Kin/Kin Customs

The customs of the Kin/Kin Relationship depend on cultural, religious, and political factors.

Kin/ Kin Two Co-partners

❼ TRAITS

Aunt/Uncle Traits

Aunt/Uncle Traits • Being Attracted

Aunt/Uncle Traits • Being Committed

Aunt/Uncle Traits • Being Genuine

Aunt/Uncle Traits • Being Trustworthy

Aunt/Uncle Traits • Being Emotionally Mature

Aunt/Uncle Traits • Having Communications Skills

Aunt/Uncle Traits • Having Problem-Solving Skills

Niece/Nephew Traits

Niece/Nephew Traits • Being Attracted

Being Attracted to your Aunt/Uncle is not an issue as far as your connectivity. She or he is your mother or father's sister/brother. Therefore, you will be interacting with them on the seesaw whether you are attracted to them or not.

If, you genuinely like your Aunt/Uncle, this can be a solid foundation for more interaction between the two of you and lead to a further development of the rest of the generic traits. Or, perhaps your Uncle/Aunt has a trade or discipline that interests you and they can help you explore your interest.

Niece/Nephew Traits • Being Committed

Your involvement with your Aunt/Uncle will determine the form of your Being Committed. If you are the only remaining relative of an aging uncle, your commitment may be to live with him until he dies. If she/he is somebody you hardly know, you may never even visit or write.

Niece/Nephew Traits • Being Genuine

As with all the Kin/Kin Relationships, your depth of Being Genuine will depend on your day-to-day involvement. If you are living together, you will want to be as genuine as possible. If you hate the person but you never see them, you will not have to call them every day to let them know your genuine feelings.

Niece/Nephew Traits • Being Trustworthy

Being Trustworthy means that you will not try to take advantage of an Aunt/Uncle who is kind to you. If she/he demonstrates trust in you such as loaning you equipment, their car, or money, you will do the right thing and return their trust with trustworthy behavior.

Niece/Nephew Traits • Having Communication Skills

Having Communication Skills will be most important when you are older and interacting with an Aunt/Uncle on a regular basis. If you are good at communicating your thoughts and feelings then your chances of being successful at this relationship are greater.

Niece/Nephew Traits • Having Problem Solving Skills

Having Problem Solving Skills is also valuable if you need to assist your Aunt/Uncle in solving a problem they are having, or you may be involved in one yourself with them. Either way, positive problem-solving skills will enhance the relation for both Co-partners.

Cousins Traits

Depending on your unique situation, you could have older cousins, the same age cousins, and/or younger cousins.

The most "normal" would be to have cousins that are near enough in age, that you could be in the same family. This means your parents have brothers or sisters who also got married and had children around the same time.

You could be the "odd" cousin by being much older or younger than the others in your family by some quirk.

Cousins Traits • Being Attracted

Cousins Traits • Being Committed

Cousins Traits • Being Genuine

Cousins Traits • Being Trustworthy

Cousins Traits • Being Emotionally Mature

Cousins Traits • Having Communications Skills

Cousins Traits • Having Problem-Solving Skills

❽ NEEDS

Aunt/Uncle Needs

Aunt/Uncle Needs • Physical

-
-

Aunt/Uncle Needs • Emotional

- To be liked
- To love the nephew/nieces

Aunt/Uncle Needs • Mental

- To be respected
- To pass on learned life skills

Aunt/Uncle Needs • Social

- Attend nephew/nieces dance recitals, school play
- To be part of the holiday family events
- Contribute to and support the family name

Niece/Nephew Needs

Niece/Nephew Needs • Physical

-
-

Niece/Nephew Needs • Emotional

- To be loved by the Aunt/Uncles
- To be fussed over or attended to by the Aunt/Uncles

Niece/Nephew Needs • Mental

- To look up to the Aunt/Uncles
- To learn from the Aunt/Uncles

Niece/Nephew Needs • Social

- To feel part of the family
- To be the future of the family

Cousin Needs

Cousin Needs • Physical

- To hang out with other cousins
- Be part of family life and interaction

Cousin Needs • Emotional

- To be accepted and loved by the other cousins as part of the family

Cousin Needs • Mental

- To be respected by the other cousins
- To teach the other cousins
- To learn from more experienced cousins

Cousin Needs • Social

- To feel part of the family
- To support financially

❾ TACTICS

Aunt/Uncle Tactics

Aunt/Uncle Tactics • Positive

Some examples of positive Tactics of Aunts/Uncle are:

- Giving birthday and holiday gifts
- Helping out with finances
- Attending school plays/graduations
- Offering help in various ways

Aunt/Uncle Tactics • Negative

Some examples of negative Tactics of the Aunts/Uncles are:

- Sexual innuendo, abuse
- Inappropriate behavior in public
- Uninvited or unwarranted advice
- Substance abuse affecting family interactions

Niece/Nephew Tactics

Niece/Nephew Tactics • Positive

Some examples of positive Tactics of Niece/Nephews are:

- Being nice to the Aunt/Uncle
- Sharing and talking about their day with the Aunt/Uncle

Niece/Nephew Tactics • Negative

Some examples of negative Tactics of the Niece/Nephews:

- Begging for gifts
- Expecting to be spoiled
- Inappropriate behavior in public
- Taking advantage of the Aunt/Uncle

Cousin Tactics

Cousin Tactics • Positive

Some examples of positive Tactics of Cousins are:

- Playing together
- Bonding
- Sharing many positive experiences

Cousin Tactics • Negative

Some examples of negative Tactics of the Cousins are:

- Sexual innuendo and/or abuse
- Inappropriate behavior in public

CHAPTER 11

*T*he Adult Child/Aging Parent Relationship

The Adult Child/Parent Relationship does not receive the attention it deserves in today's Western society. This relationship is not even discussed by many relationship "experts." What seems to go unnoticed is that as children mature they no longer are at the mercy of their parents. This completely changes the dynamics of the original Parent/Child Relationship. These complex issues will receive more attention as the Baby-Boomers ascend to the age where these issues become a prominent aspect of their lives.

Adult freedoms and rights were simply unavailable to the child in the Parent/Child Relationship. Typically the transition in age or rights goes unnoticed by the Co-partners. They simply continue the dynamics of the Parent/Child Relationship they both had when younger.

But conditions have changed. Now the Adult Child has rights and responsibilities in society's eyes and can't be protected by the parents. After a few more years go by the Aging Parent is in a slow decline. He or she will eventually need taking care of just like a child.

If these changes in status and freedoms are not acknowledged by the Co-partners, they may continue to function under the same operating system of roles and rules that existed when they were younger. An extreme example is the story of the 80-year-old mother who didn't want her 60-year-old daughter dating a certain man.

With the advancement of age also comes the changing of the guard. Parents can no longer be the active protectors of the children. The Aging Parents will become old, feeble, hard of hearing and weak of sight. They will need taking care of and this responsibility falls to the children. These changes mean the Adult Child becomes the dominant Co-partner in the relationship, which is why his/her role is now placed first in the relationship name.

The question arises, when does the Child start becoming the Adult Child? HRW suggests that between the ages of 20 to 40 for the child is when the Adult Child/Aging Parent Relationships begins to come into play.

For a few years the Parent/Child Relationship could begin functioning more like a Friend/Friend Relationship. Both Co-partners are ideally healthy and mobile and their interaction is based on their mutual attraction and respect.

In particular, the Adult Child must evaluate if the current status of the relationship is positive, friendly, and mutually supportive. If it's not, then this is when changes need to be made.

The next question is when do the full dynamics of the Adult Child/Parent Relationship come into force? An arbitrary definition point could be when the Aging Parents hit 60. From this point on, the Adult Child can be thinking ahead with these dynamics in mind.

Adult Child/Aging Parent Environment

The Environment of the Adult Child/Parent Relationship is a key factor because of its many possible variations. More than any other, the major problems that crop up in this relationship can be based on the Environment alone. For example, as parents become older they may be considered for a retirement home or community which they may resist or perhaps prefer. This change is environmental in nature.

❶ LOCATION

First of all, where does your Aging Parent live and what kind of circumstances is he/she living under. How old are your parents? Are both parents still alive and functioning normally? Has one parent recently died, putting extreme duress on the other? Have any health circumstances occurred that make the current Location no longer appropriate? Is the distance between the Co-partners becoming a negative? Are any aspects of the Location, such as stairs or size of the residence, becoming a problem?

Another factor of the Location is that whoever is the Adult Child living closest to the presumably still married parents will be the de facto choice for emergency decisions. And what if the parents are divorced and living in different parts of the country or world?

When the Adult Child is between 20 and 40

Due to economic realities and other causes, many children are moving back into the parent's home which presents various problems for each Co-partner. What happens when the Adult Child is still living in the same location the Co-partners shared during the primary Parent/Child Relationship? In this situation, the dynamics are unlikely to change from their earlier Parent/Child Relationship. Is "mom" still doing the wash and making the bed? Is the daughter still living at home without paying rent and spending all her money on clothes, make-up, and boys even as she approaches 30?

When the Adult Child is over 40

This is when the Location factors become more important for the Aging Parent. The Adult Child must begin to analyze the Aging Parent's living circumstances for factors that are impacting the aging parents and the relationship itself.

❷ DURATION

The Duration of the Adult Child/Adult Parent Relationship will remain a biological fact as long as both Co-partners remain alive. In practical terms, the Duration is based on whether or not the Co-partners still spend time communicating and interacting with each other. If the Co-partners are estranged, they may never come in contact. In this situation the relationship has ceased to exist for all intents and purposes.

❸ TIMING

The Timing of the Adult Child/Adult Parent Relationship may vary considerably. The adults may see or talk to each other on a daily basis, talk on the phone every two or three months, or refrain from contact for years.

It's important to keep in mind that the Timing for the Adult Child/Aging Parent Relationship would only be counted when this is the correct seesaw that is being expressed as opposed to bigger family or social gatherings such as Christmas or Hanukah.

Adult Child/Aging Parent Structure

Adult children tend to stay in touch with their parents despite distance, social mobility, or clashes over basic values. This is based on the universal observation, "You only have one set of parents." The main form of contact would be the phone or home visits during which the Co-partners chat about each other's well-being, share general news, and attend family holiday gatherings. Talk is not necessarily intimate and certain aspects of life may be excluded. There is more tangible and obligatory help in this relationship than any other except marriage.

❹ ROLES

Adult Child Role

By definition the Adult Child should be fully independent of his/her parents. This means living on his/her own and financially out from under the wings of the parents. The Adult Child may be married, living with someone, or living alone. If married, they may have already started a family, producing grandchildren for their parents.

When this has been accomplished, the Adult Child is now an equal or peer to the parent in certain ways that did not exist when the Adult Child was younger. It may be important for the Adult Child to communicate this understanding with the parents if circumstances warrant it.

The Role of the Adult Child is to love, support, and nurture his/her parents in any way that seems appropriate. Once the child reaches adulthood, if the relation has taken on more of the characteristics of a good friendship and the relationship is mutually supportive, the transition has been successful.

If the relationship is unhappy and toxic, the Adult Child must take steps to correct the situation. The Adult Child should not feel burdened by responsibilities that the Aging Parents will not assume for themselves.

Adult Child Roles • Physical

Physically, the Role of the Adult Child is to help the Aging Parent when assistance is necessary, such as:

- Mowing the lawn
- Cleaning the house
- Providing transportation
- Taking care of finances
- Managing daily affairs
- Monitoring health and fitness

Adult Child Roles • Emotional

Emotionally, the Role of the Adult Child is to:

- Love and support the Aging Parent
- Spend time with the Aging Parent
- Show interest in the Aging Parent's daily life
- Share daily discourse with the Aging Parent
- Show appreciation and respect for the Aging Parent

Adult Child Roles • Mental

Mentally, the Role of the Adult Child is to:

- Provide help with mental tasks if needed
- Pay attention to changing conditions of the Aging Parents
- Protect the Aging Parents from scams

Adult Child Roles • Social

Socially, the Role of the Adult Child is to:

- Engage, in social activities with Aging Parents
- Assist the Aging Parents in attending their social activities as needed

Aging Parent Role

The Aging Parent is often a completely different person than he/she was 20 to 40 years earlier. He or she has often settled many issues plaguing the childbearing years such as marriage or career issues, thus earning a place in society and hopefully establishing financial independence.

Negative patterns that were prominent in the parent from the ages of 20 to 60 may be completely changed, such as violent outbursts, workaholism, or other negative behaviors. This can be frustrating for the Adult Child since he/she was the brunt of these behaviors which people in your parent's current life have never seen and could never believe.

Some Aging Parents are able to view their children as adults and equals. However, others are often unable to accept that they have lost the reign of power they once enjoyed. The perceived success or failure of the Adult Child in society (by the Aging Parent) may also play a significant role in the current relationship.

Activities your parents once performed, like shopping, may now be tiring or even difficult for them. They may find these limitations painful as well as embarrassing. Other factors that will surely come as the parents age are the loss of health and physical fitness.

Aging Parent Roles • Physical

Physically, the Role of the Aging Parent is to:

- Not be an undue burden to the Adult Child
- Contribute financially, if able
- Take care of self as much as possible
- Maintain an active and healthy lifestyle

Aging Parent Roles • Emotional

Emotionally, the Role of the Aging Parent is to:

- Let go of prior power position
- Increasingly view the Adult child as his/her own person

- Seek to loosen the ties of the prior Parent/Child Relationship
- Love and support the Adult Child
- Accept Adult Child as an equal

Aging Parent Roles • Mental

Mentally, the Role of the Aging Parent is to:

- Take care of future eventualities, such as prepare a will
- Respect the Adult child as his/her own person
- Respect and support the Adult Child's lifestyle choices
- Choose a successor to be the Executor of your estate

Aging Parent Roles • Social

Socially, the Role of the Aging Parent is to:

- Take part in family celebrations
- Be willing to pass the family torch

❺ RULES

Adult Child Rules

Adult Child Rules • Physical

Physically, the Rules of the Adult Child are to:

- Be watchful of the Aging Parent's health needs
- Arrange for Aging Parent's health and personal care if necessary
- Monitor the living conditions and daily maintenance of the Aging Parent
- Make a safety check of the Aging Parent's house, such as bright enough illumination, dangerous throw rugs, a higher toilet seat, etc
- Arrange for Aging Parent's daily needs such as food, exercise, and basic shopping

Adult Child Rules • Emotional

Emotionally, the Rules of the Adult Child are to:

- Begin separating the new patterns of the Adult Child/Aging Parent Relationship from the old patterns of the prior Parent/Child Relationship
- Leave home at an appropriate time to achieve and establish independence
- Be watchful for invasive or negative acts by the Aging Parent
- Never tell Aging Parents they are "over the hill"
- Ask about your Aging Parents friends and support system

Adult Child Rules • Mental

Mentally, the Rules of the Adult Child are to:

- Make sure Aging Parent is competent to handle finances
- Discuss financial "what if" strategies, such as a durable power of attorney
- Discuss funeral and burial preferences
- Make sure the Aging Parent files claims for all medical bills
- Be prepared to spend time, money, and personal visits to assist Aging Parent
- Not feel burdened or obligated by responsibilities that the Adult Parents can, but won't, assume for themselves

Adult Child Rules • Social

Socially, the Rules of the Adult Child are to:

- Include the Aging Parents in on family and social events as much as practical
- Keep in touch with Aging Parent's support system, such as friends, neighbors, church or _____?

Aging Parent Rules

The rules for the Aging Parent will be based around the age of the Aging Parent.

Aging Parent Rules • Physical

Physically, the Aging Parent should:

- Take care of physical needs
- Have fun
- Maintain health
- Be exercising
- Eat healthy foods
- Get regular health check-ups

Aging Parent Rules • Emotional

Emotionally, the Aging Parent should:

- Don't worry, be happy
- Accept current life, not "what could have been"
- Strive to find purposeful activities
- Follow feelings more
- Consider fulfilling personal dreams he/she may have put off when younger

Aging Parent Rules • Mental

Mentally, the Aging Parent should:

- Develop outside interests and hobbies
- Be open about financial situation and "what if" health circumstances
- Prepare a list of all income and assets
- Prepare a valid will
- Consider a living will, so as not to live in a vegetative state
- Consider setting up online transfers for paying bills and receiving income

Aging Parent Rules • Social

Socially, the Aging Parent should:

- Identify your current support system, such as friends, neighbors, church or temple, doctors, etc
- Keep names and addresses of support system current
- Cooperate with Adult Child in planning for future eventualities

❻ CUSTOMS

Adult Child Customs

Customs are the major area that determines how the elderly are treated. In Japanese and Chinese culture for example, the elderly are treated with the utmost respect. In American culture, the elderly are tossed aside like a bad smell.

Adult Child Customs • Cultural

Adult Child Customs • Religious

Adult Child Customs • Political

Aging Parent Customs

Customs of the Aging Parent Relationship truly depend on your culture of origin.

Aging Parent Customs • Cultural

Aging Parent Customs • Religious

Aging Parent Customs • Political

Adult Child/Aging Parent Co-partners

The success of the Adult Child/Aging Parent Relationship is going to depend on the traits of the Co-partners. If both Co-partners are mature with communication and problem-solving skills, the relationship will bring added dimension to each others lives. If either Co-partner is immature and unwilling to accept the realities of their situation, this relationship can be an ongoing source of stress for both. Adult Children and Aging Parents usually feel affection for each other and enjoy each other's company. The tendency is to be closer with the mother than the father.

❼ TRAITS

Adult Child Traits

The Adult Child must be willing to shoulder more and more responsibility for the Aging Parents. Difficult decisions will be forthcoming in many areas. Depending on family dynamics (is this person an only child, one of eight children, etc.) these responsibilities can provide an additional burden on an already stressful situation. These conditions are guaranteed to challenge the integrity of the Adult Child traits.

Adult Child Traits • Being Attracted

Ideally, you will like and respect your Aging Parents. If this is the case, you will be attracted to them and be happy to participate in their lives as well as them in yours. If you live close to them it will be much easier and practical to keep in touch and interact. If you dislike your Aging Parents, you will find it difficult to interact with them. In this case you might find yourself in uncomfortable circumstances when you must take part in family functions or if the responsibility for their welfare falls fully on you.

Adult Child Traits • Being Committed

Being Committed is your ability to perform the duties of the Adult Child no matter what your personal preferences. This trait insures that you meet the needs and wants of your Aging Parents to the best of your ability. As a matter of reciprocity, you owe your parents whatever they truly need.

Adult Child Traits • Being Genuine

Being Genuine means communicating your exact thoughts and feelings, without being personally spiteful. If something true needs to be said, you will not hide or shirk your duty, such as bringing up difficult subject areas like failing health, financial problems, or funeral plans.

Adult Child Traits • Being Trustworthy

Being Trustworthy is your ability to watch out for your Aging Parents and not take advantage of their failing health and mental faculties. You will do what is right by them to the best of your ability and endeavor to protect them from unscrupulous people who prey on the aging.

Adult Child Traits • Being Emotionally Mature

Being Emotionally Mature is your ability to handle the problems and situation that are inevitable as the relationship progresses. You will he challenged by many difficult decisions and complicated circumstances, especially if other siblings are involved. Also involved will be your mixed bag of emotions and feelings concerning the state of your parents as well as how this impacts your personal lifestyle.

Adult Child Traits • Having Communication Skills

Having Communication Skills will benefit you highly; even more so since communicating effectively with your parents can be one of life's most difficult tasks. Ideally, you will have already established open and honest pathways of communication. If not, you will have the double difficulty of confronting communication patterns that go back to your childhood as well as working to resolve current problems and situations that will arise.

Adult Child Traits • Having Problem-Solving Skills

Communication and Problem-Solving Skills go hand in hand. If your Aging Parents are still at the age where they are competent to handle their own decisions, you can simply monitor them in this regard. If, through disease or increasing age, they become unable to perform their normal duties, then you will be obligated to take a more active role in resolving not only your problems together, but the problems they may have with other outside parties.

Aging Parent Traits

The Traits of the Aging Parent aren't likely to improve as time goes on. If anything, difficult traits are likely to worsen. The Aging Parent's logic is that he or she has been that way so long, why change now. Losing physical or mental faculties can also cause dramatic changes in states of mind very quickly. Any negative change in the condition of the Aging Parent adds directly to the responsibilities of the Adult Child.

Aging Parent Traits • Being Attracted

Depending on the mutual level of love, trust, and respect for your Adult child, the trait of Being Attracted will be strong or weak. If you have a positive relationship with your Adult Children and their family members, you will be respected and honored for your position as a family leader. If your relationship with your Adult Children is difficult or estranged, you may see them rarely, if ever.

Aging Parent Traits • Being Committed

Being Committed is your willingness to help and assist your Adult Child which could take many forms. You may live with them and participate in family management. You may only see your Adult Child for two weeks during the summer or at holidays.

Each Aging Parent establishes his/her own person level of commitment to the relationship. As your faculties wane, you must allow your affairs to be increasingly handled by the younger family members.

Aging Parent Traits • Being Genuine

Your ability to Be Genuine will have been established long before your relationship with your Adult Children. It is unlikely that you will change your essential style of Being Genuine during the later years of your life. Whatever you were like before, is how you will function now.

Aging Parent Traits • Being Trustworthy

Being Trustworthy is another trait that is unlikely to change in your later years. If you have established a relationship of trust and respect with your children, this will likely continue.

Aging Parent Traits • Being Emotionally Mature

For most people, emotional maturity comes with age. You will have many situations as an Aging Parent that will test your ability to "go with the flow" in a mature manner. As different choices arise, you will be well-served if you can react to them in a sensible, mature manner.

Aging Parent Traits • Having Communication Skills

Communication skills are vital to explain your needs and wants to your Adult Children. These abilities will smooth your children's transition out of the nest as well as support your personal circumstances and decisions as your life evolves.

Aging Parent Traits • Having Problem-Solving Skills

Having Problem-Solving Skills will help you to resolve family disputes. As the patriarch or matriarch of your family, you may be asked for your advice and counsel. The many varieties of situations that can arise when dealing with family issues will require a fair and honest understanding of conflict-resolution methods.

❽ NEEDS

Adult Child Needs

The needs of the Adult Child will be basically to allocate time and resources to your Adult Child/Aging Parent Relationship without draining the personal resources you need to maintain your own life.

Adult Child Needs • Physical

Physically, the needs of the Adult Child are to:

- Have own home and environment
- Be financially independent
- Be free of undue constrictions on time and energy

Adult Child Needs • Emotional

Emotionally, the needs of the Adult Child are to:

- Not be emotionally suffocated by Aging Parents
- Be emotionally independent and secure
- Feel love and compassion for Aging Parents

Adult Child Needs • Mental

Mentally, the needs of the Adult Child are to:

- Develop own career and life decisions
- Be able to live the lifestyle he/she prefers
- Know that in just a few years what's going on with your Adult Parents will probably be happening to you

Adult Child Needs • Social

Socially, the needs of the Adult Child are to:

- Be part of a larger family group
- Have the support of extended family
- Consider the special needs the Aging Parents might have to maintain their schedules and/or lifestyles.

Aging Parent Needs

Your needs as the Aging Parent will be specific to your age and energy level. Perhaps you are looking forward to your Adult Children being on their own so you and your spouse can pursue your own activities. Maybe your age or condition of health is so advanced that you need care and monitoring around the clock.

Aging Parent Needs • Physical

Physically, the needs of the Aging Parent are to:

– Be healthy and receive quality medical care
– Eat, exercise, and sleep properly
– Have finances in order

Aging Parent Needs • Emotional

Emotionally, the needs of the Aging Parent are to:

– Be loved and respected by Adult Child
– Share in family interactions
– Be appreciated as family elders

Aging Parent Needs • Mental

Mentally, the needs of the Aging Parent are to:

– Develop own interests and hobbies
– Travel or seek to meet other lifetime goals
– Spend time in a useful and meaningful manner

Aging Parent Needs • Social

Socially, the needs of the Aging Parent are to:

– Be part of a larger family group
– Have the support of extended family

❾ TACTICS

Adult Child Tactics

Tactics are the ways that a Co-partner uses to meet his/her needs. In the Adult Child/Aging Parent Relationship the Adult Child must be thinking of ways to meet the needs of both Co-partners. This can be one of Life's most difficult challenges.

Adult Child Tactics • Positive

Some examples of positive tactics are:

- Consulting with Aging Parents over difficult decisions
- Staying in regular communication with Aging Parents
- Being respectful and considerate of Aging Parent's desires
- Taking responsibility for difficult decisions
- Discuss various options of aging care with Aging Parent

Adult Child Tactics • Negative

Some examples of negative tactics are:

- Making life altering decisions without consulting or informing Aging Parents
- Evicting parents from the home they gave you
- Cleaning out Aging Parents bank accounts

Aging Parent Tactics

Aging Parent Tactics • Positive

Some examples of positive tactics for the Aging Parent are:

- Have wills, and trusts and legal documents in place while still having mental faculties
- Consider transitional stages with Adult Child before their needs become urgent

- Being willing to plan for the future and take needed actions before becoming a burden
- Accept the future as it appears and not resist the inevitable
- Explain your desires and pick your successors

Aging Parent Tactics • Negative

Some examples of negative tactics for the Aging Parent are:

- Refusing to even consider wills, and trusts and legal documents
- Refusing needed medical treatment or such things as hearing aids, reading glasses, or walking support
- Resisting any attempts by Adult Child and/or other family members to discuss or implement plans for the future
- Being fully convinced you are never going to die
- Keeping secrets that impact other family members

PART TWO: SECTION TWO

INTRO TO
SOCIAL RELATIONSHIPS

CHAPTER 12

*T*he Friend/Friend Relationship

Friends are people who like each other, enjoy participating in activities together, and are not blood relatives. Friends are important to both sexes, in every age group, from all cultures. Most people derive extreme satisfaction from their friendships.

As well as being a major source of leisure, Friend/Friend Relationships provide positive many positive health benefits. People with more friends are happier, healthier, and live longer. The Friend/Friend Relationship is the best choice to begin learning the dynamics of HRW as it provides an easy entry into the deeper power and structures of HRW.

Two sociological groups derive the most benefit from Friend/Friend Relationships.

Younger People

Friend/Friend Relationships are of primary importance to teenagers and adults until they marry. For this group, the focus consists of mutual activities such as going out to eat, attending movies, or going to clubs. For younger people especially, friendships involve meeting socially and are entertainment oriented.

Older People

In later life, friends help each other by acting as confidantes. They also ease the stress of bereavement or retirement and as companions, minimize the effects of loneliness.

Friend/Friend Environment

The Environment provides the essential character of the Friend/Friend Relationship since friends seek the environments that they mutually enjoy. The initiating factor of a Friend/Friend Relationship is often a chance environmental proximity. Simply by being present in the same environment of interest, two people may meet and become friends.

❶ LOCATION

Any location can be the setting for a Friend/Friend Relationship and the Location can vary. Friends may live across the street, attend the same school, work at the same location, live in the same town, exercise at the same club, ride the same bus, or go to the same beach. The environmental factors of friendship are also reflective of the socio-economic, cultural, and religious influences in each Co-partner's life.

❷ DURATION

Duration is the quantity of elapsed time the relationship has existed. The Duration of a Friend/Friend Relationship can be from one night to a lifetime. A best friend relationship must obviously have extended duration to qualify as a best friend relationship. Some factors involving the Environment that have an impact on Duration are moving away, leaving school after graduation, and changes in family or work situations that are out of the Co-partners control.

❸ TIMING

For younger people, the Timing of the Friend/Friend Relationship is often based on social activities, such as movies, parties, or other social functions. These might typically involve nighttime activities, such as going to a restaurant, clubs, or dancing. For older people, the Timing typically involves more daytime activities such as getting together for coffee, shopping, or volunteer work.

Friend/Friend Structure

The Role for a Co-partner in the Friend/Friend Structure is simply to "hang out" and do things together. Friends share experiences with each other and, in turn, give each other social support. The Role and Rules in this structure are identical for both Co-partners. Friends are non-judgmental as well as understanding, honest, and caring.

Friends help each other to reminisce about old experiences, understand new ones, and cope with life's current situations. Friends discuss their personal lives with each other as well as give and receive advice. Since Friends enjoy each other's company, they often share leisure, common interests and social activities.

Because friends are helpful and understanding, they feel comfortable with each other. Their emotions, desires, and motives are often similar. They share feelings of love and respect for each other. Friends show concern for each other's welfare as well as loyalty and commitment to the relationship structure.

Friendship includes the willingness to share activities and companionship. Not only are friends supportive and cooperative emotionally, they are willing to assist and teach each other. They can also be trusted to volunteer help in time of need.

❹ ROLES

Categories of Friends: Intimacy and Gender

The Roles of the Friend/Friend Relationship can be further evaluated by intimacy and gender. These categories are:

- Best Friends
- Acquaintances
- Same Sex: Female/Female
- Same Sex: Male/Male
- Opposite Sex Friends (???)

Intimacy is the dividing measure of friendship. The more two people know about each other, the better friends they become. When their level of intimacy and trust with each other becomes unique, they are best friends.

Best Friends

Best friends discuss more intimate topics, give more help, and feel more relaxed in each others company. Your best friend is also the one most likely to tell you something, even if it hurts. It is only possible to have one best friend or, at the most, two closest friends. It's possible that for you, a person is your best friend, but for the other person, he/she has someone that is his/her best friend and/or vice versa.

Acquaintances

Acquaintances can be friends that are more specific to one area of your life, perhaps school or outside interests such as car repair or pottery. They can be quite strong in defined areas, but the value and commitment of the relationship overall is less than a best friend.

One measure of an Acquaintance would be how much they know about you or how much you are willing to divulge to him/her. An Acquaintance might also be your best friend during a set period of time (lost on a desert island perhaps), but then some aspect of the environment changes and the friendship doesn't endure.

Same Sex: Female/Female Friend Relationship

Female friends spend much of their time together giving and receiving social support. Their relationships involve a high degree of self-disclosure and discussion of personal problems. They often act as mutual confidantes and therapists. Women value intimate, confidential relationships, affection, and social support. Women like to discuss children, personal problems, work issues, other men, and sports. According to studies, both men and women say that their friendships with women are superior to those with men.

Same Sex: Male/Male Friend Relationship

The friends in Male/Male Relationships primarily share activities. They may play games, compete in sports, or engage in leisure activities, such as jogging, tennis, or hunting. Male friendships are less emotionally intimate. Men are more likely than women to belong to structured groups and clubs engaged in worthwhile tasks. Men enjoy discussing work, other women, sports, goals for the future, and their families.

Opposite Sex Relationships

A true Opposite Sex friendship is difficult to establish and maintain. In fact, from the point of view of generic human studies, they don't exist. The biggest difficulty is the potential for the eventual emergence of sexual feelings which, technically speaking, are not an aspect of this relationship.

For all those women out there who say that they have plenty of male friends, I have two questions.

- 1) Would any of your male "friends" have sex with you if you said okay?
- 2) Where are all the female friends you don't have?

Maybe you have some girlfriends that you go out with to hunt guys and than ditch each other as soon as you meet someone.

And, for the guys:

- 1) How many girl "friends" do you have that you wouldn't have sex with?
- 2) How many of these "friends" aren't:
    - A school friend
    - A Neighbor
    - In-laws
    - People you know from work
    - Linked more to someone else in your life

If not, why do you hang around and do things with this person?

Shared intimacies tend to increase closeness. When two friends of the same sex discuss intimate details of their personal lives (their courting or marriage problems, for example), they share the experience only. If a male and female "friend" confide in each other about their courting or marriage problems, an intimacy can occur which causes the other person to appear sexually attractive.

Successful Opposite Sex Friend/Friend Relationships could only occur if sexual interaction is completely ruled out. An example might be if one or both Co-partners are 100% gay. Or when the two friends have already had a sexual relationship which has ended in which case they are in an Ex-lover/Ex-lover Friendship, and again not a true friendship.

Religious or moral beliefs might once have irrefutably ruled out any sexual interaction (although sexual chemistry would still exist) between the two individuals of the opposite sex, but this no longer appears to be the case.

The Opposite Sex Friend/Friend Relationship is a troublesome relationship to establish and tenuous at best. Even if it works for some strange reason, once either Co-partner gets a serious dating partner or becomes married, the other person's Co-partner will break up the party.

And when a husband or wife says, "My spouse is my best friend." Not so. Your spouse is your spouse. There are certain things that you could easily tell your best friend that you better not be saying in front of your spouse.

Friend Role

Friend Role • Physical

Physically, the Role of a Friend is to:

- Spend time and do things together
- Volunteer help when you need it
- Not have sex

Friend Role • Emotional

Emotionally, the Role of a Friend is to:

- Show interest in each other's daily activities
- Disclose personal feelings or problems to each other
- Share news of success
- Be sensitive to each other's emotional needs
- Be concerned enough to ask if there is a problem
- Strive to make each other happy in their company
- Be able to share their deepest thoughts arid feelings
- Allow each other the freedom to express feelings without being judged

Friend Role • Mental

Mentally, the Role of a Friend is to:

- Stay in touch and communicate
- Trust and confide in each other
- Ask each other for personal advice
- Be understanding
- Communicate their needs to each other
- Respect each other's privacy
- Not nag each other
- Not judge each other negatively
- Keep confidences
- Explore mutual interests together
- Teach and share knowledge
- Help each other resolve problems and differences
- Keep each other informed on matters that affect them

Friend Role • Social

Socially, the Role of a Friend is to:

- Join each other in social activities
- Not use or take undue advantage of each other
- Not overstay welcome or take advantage of hospitality

- Pay back borrowed money
- Repay favors, and compliments
- Engage in joking or teasing with each other
- Not ridicule or criticize the other in public
- Be supportive of each other in their absence
- Be tolerant of each other's friends.
- Not be jealous or critical of friend's other relationships

❺ RULES

Friend Rules

The Rules of Friend/Friend Relationships closely follow their Role responsibilities. If a person doesn't act in accordance with the Rules of friendship, then he or she is not your friend.

Friend Rules • Physical

Physically, the Rules of a Friend are to:

- Spend time and do things together
- Volunteer help when you need it
- Not have sex

Friend Rules • Emotional

Emotionally, the Rules of a Friend are to:

- Show interest in each other's daily activities
- Disclose personal. Feelings or problems to each other
- Share news of success
- Be sensitive to each other's emotional needs
- Be concerned enough to ask if there is a problem
- Strive to make each other happy in their company
- Be able to share their deepest thoughts and feelings
- Allow each other the freedom to express feelings without being judged

Friend Rules • Mental

Mentally, the Rules of a Friend are to:

- Stay in touch and communicate
- Trust and confide in each other
- Ask each other for personal advice
- Be understanding
- Communicate their needs to each other
- Respect each other's privacy
- Not nag each other
- Not judge each other negatively
- Keep confidences
- Explore mutual interests together
- Teach and share knowledge
- Help each other resolve problems and differences
- Keep each other informed on matters that affect them

Friend Rules • Social

Socially, the Rules of a Friend are to:

- Join each other in social activities
- Not use or take undue advantage of each other
- Not overstay welcome or take advantage of hospitality
- Pay back borrowed money
- Repay favors, and compliments
- Engage in joking or teasing with
- Not ridicule or criticize each other in public
- Be supportive of each other in their absence
- Be tolerant of each other's friends.
- Not be jealous or critical of friend's other relationships

❻ CUSTOMS

The Customs of Friend/Friend Relationships depend on cultural, religious, and political factors.

Friend Customs • Cultural

Leisure activities seem to be universal between friends, such as:

- Eating together
- Playing sports
- Attending movies

Other Customs associated with Friend/Friend Relationships in western culture are:

- Going to social and cultural events
- Travelling or going on vacations together

Friend Customs • Religious

Some religious customs are:

-
-

Friend Customs • Political

Some Political Customs among friends are:

- If your friend is breaking the law, pardon him
-

Friend/Friend Co-partners

Your Best Friend is the person of the same sex whom you trust and confide in the most. He/she is that one person you can trust to be there for you. Acquaintances are those people you know but with whom you lack the shared intimacies associated with best friends. You could have many acquaintances with varying degrees of closeness and intimacy.

You might have various reasons to call a particular person a friend. Perhaps the way he/she plays the guitar. Maybe they are the only person you know who likes going to Las Vegas. Having a certain friend for a certain reason is possible and ultimately practical in many ways.

The HRW traits might not be the main reason you have or like a particular friend. They do tell you who your best friends are and which friendships will be the most stress free. Your friends with positive HRW traits will be the friendships that last over time.

❼ TRAITS

Friend Traits • Being Attracted

Attraction is a key component of friendship. How much you like and want to be with the other person is fully one-half of the exchange. If you mutually respect each other and enjoy being together, you have the all-important trait of attraction to keep you both on the relationship seesaw. "Hanging out" and doing nothing is still fun.

Friend Traits • Being Committed

Commitment is measured by the time and energy friends put into their relationship. If either are lacking, the relationship will be weak. Although friends can often maintain the same intensity of feelings without seeing each other for years, commitment by HRW standards means contacting or communicating with each other at least once per month.

Friend Traits • Being Genuine

Being genuine or emotionally sincere is another measure of friendship. If you cannot be honest with your best friend, then you cannot be honest with anyone, including yourself. A friend is your peer and the one in whom you must be able to confide your deepest intimacies. If you can't tell your best friend your innermost thoughts and feelings, who can you tell?

Friend Traits • Being Trustworthy

Keeping agreements is a very important aspect of all human relationships, but it is especially crucial in the Friend/Friend Relationship. The ideal Co-partner is trustworthy and dependable. If a friend tells you that he/she will meet you at 7:00 and they don't show up until 9:00 or not at all, how trustworthy is this friend? Is your friend always there for you and you for your friend? If so, this speaks well for your positive traits.

Friend Traits • Being Emotionally Mature

Emotional Maturity is the Trait of behaving in a way that is responsible to the needs of both people in the relationship. As a child or young adult, maturity is not the highest priority for establishing friendships.

Friend/Friend Relationships can be based more on attraction and circumstances. As one grows older, emotional maturity and dependability becomes a more important element of the Friend/Friend Relationship. Mature friends are not jealous, spiteful, or negative to each other.

Friend Traits • Having Communication Skills

Having Communication Skills is the ability to communicate your thoughts and feelings as well as listen to the thoughts and feelings of others. In Best Friend Relationships this Trait is not as crucial because they are empathic already. The most important factor of communication is the intimacy and feeling of connection that best friends share Do you feel comfortable when communicating with your friend as opposed to awkward, uncomfortable, or embarrassed? Communication Skills are particularly important when you believe an unacknowledged change has occurred in your relationship. You must communicate about this situation or you will continue to experience awkward feelings in your relationship.

Friend Traits • Having Problem-Solving

Problem-Solving Skills help tremendously in Friend/Friend Relationships because even best friends can experience conflicts. This Trait increases in importance as friends get older. Even if your Friend/Friend Relationship never experiences conflict, the advice of a friend skilled in problem-solving can always help sort out problems you might have in other relationships. The value of a true friend can be measured by his/her ability to help you solve problems you have with others.

❸ NEEDS

People have different friends for different reasons. Your needs as a Co-partner in the Friend/Friend Relationship are a replica of the roles and rules contained in the Structure (Roles, Rules, Customs) of the Friend/Friend Relationship.

The importance and value of friendship is that your Needs are met by someone that you spend time with and share activities. This person cares about your physical, emotional, mental, and social welfare.

Friend Needs • Physical

Physically, you need friends to:

- Spend time and do things with you
- Volunteer help when you need it
- Assist with short term loans or other help
- Help you with physical chores such as moving or building
- Watch your back

Friend Needs • Emotional

Emotionally, you need friends to:

- Show interest in your daily activities
- Disclose personal feelings or problems to
- Share news of success
- Be sensitive to your emotional needs
- Be concerned enough to ask if there is a problem
- Strive to make you happy in their company
- Be able to share your deepest thoughts and feelings
- Allow you the freedom to express feelings without being judged

Friend Needs • Mental

Mentally, you need friends to:

- Stay in touch and communicate
- Trust and confide in
- Ask for personal advice
- Be understanding
- Communicate your needs to respect your privacy
- Not nag you
- Not judge you negatively
- Keep confidences
- Explore your interests together
- Teach and share knowledge
- Help you resolve problems and differences
- Keep you informed on matters that affect each other

Friend Needs • Social

Socially, you need friends to:

- Join you in social activities
- Not use or take undue advantage of you
- Not overstay welcome or take advantage of hospitality
- Pay back borrowed money

- Repay favors, and compliments
- Engage in joking or teasing with
- Not ridicule or criticize you in public
- Be supportive of you in your absence
- Be tolerant of your friends.
- Not be jealous or critical of your other relationships

❾ TACTICS

Tactics are the ways and means that both friends use to get their needs met. As in any relationship, the Co-partners may employ positive and/or negative tactics.

Friend Tactics • Positive

Friends use positive tactics to enhance the meeting of each other's needs. Some examples are:

- Initiating communication
- Calling or writing your friends
- Sharing concerns with them
- Asking about his/her life
- Talking about your life
- Sharing news with each other
- Asking about problems
- Expressing loyalty and commitment
- Discussing dreams, goals, and priorities
- Being honest and open
- Being an empathic listener
- Showing loyalty
- Giving encouragement
- Sharing activities
- Engage in activities together
- Having parties
- Going to the movies
- Watching television

- Going camping, sailing, or swimming
- Having picnics
- Playing sports
- Spending time
  - Evenings
  - Days
  - Weekends
  - Vacations
- Doing things for each other
- Bringing gifts
- Paying compliments
- Doing favors

Friend Tactics • Negative

Negative Tactics reflect the opposite of the positive tactics and, when used, weaken or destroy the bonds of the relationship. Some examples are:

- Always second guessing your friends motives
- Making light of his/her compliments
- Making promise you don't keep
- Altering the meaning of your friend's comments
- Accusing your friend of trying to insult you
- Not following through on commitments
- Not making time to spend with your friend
- Putting other people or things (such as work) in front of your friendship
- Not returning phone calls or letters
- Continually canceling lunch or dinner dates
- Ditching plans with your friend for new dating opportunities

Introducing the Boyfriend/Girlfriend Relationships

The Boyfriend/Girlfriend Relationship is possibly the most "popular" relationship in that most people, if you mentioned you were reading a book on "how relationships work," would assume you were referring to the Boyfriend/Girlfriend Relationship. It takes some people quite a while before they consider a sibling, a neighbor, or a Coworker as involving "a relationship." However, for the next four chapters, we are going to discuss the Boyfriend/Girlfriend Relationship exclusively.

Although it may not appear so on the surface, the basic elements of courting behavior are similar throughout the world. Whether the roles are filled by Romeo and Juliet, Rhett Butler and Scarlet O'Hara or you and your dating partner, the different qualities of each Co-partner along with the high stakes of biological perpetuation provide the universal drama associated with the Boyfriend/Girlfriend Relationship.

The Boyfriend/Girlfriend Relationship is the relationship of human mate selection. It forms the biological platform for mating and continuation of the species. Another word that communicates the activities associated with the Boyfriend/Girlfriend Relationship is courting.

The Boyfriend/Girlfriend Relationships begin the transition between past and future generations which the prior generation's Husband/Wife Relationship began by creating a new generation of

Parent/Child Relationships. Generically speaking, the high stakes of the Boyfriend/Girlfriend Relationships boil down to the survival of the species.

The Boyfriend/Girlfriend Relationship is fiercely competitive. It begins with males competing against males for available females and ends with competition between male and female for dominance within their relationship.

Courting signals come pre-wired in the brain. They occur below conscious awareness in a deep part of the brain stem known as the vestibular level. If you removed the entire cerebral cortex, the outer covering of your brain, you would still court, have sex, and parent. You would not be able to think or reason, but you could still court and have sex.

There Is More Than One Stage of a Boyfriend/Girlfriend Relationship

Before describing this relationship in detail, I would like to make some points that don't seem to fit in anywhere else.

It turns out that the "Boyfriend/'Girlfriend Relationship" can be a bit complicated, as there are three distinct stages this relationship goes through. Each of these stages is so different they each have their own chapter in HRW, even though technically they are only a single stage in the progression of a generic Boyfriend/Girlfriend Relationship. Each stage has its own chapter so its dynamics and variations can be illustrated using the HRW Relationship Model.

Another interesting aspect is the first and third stages of the Boyfriend/Girlfriend Relationship are transition stages. The second stage of dating one Co-partner exclusively is where most people would categorize this relation. However, the first stage is in preparation for the second. And the third stage is designed for transition to the Husband/Wife Relationship.

Each stage has its own set of dynamics and booby traps, along with various stage-specific challenges. Please keep a clear mind as you read the following three chapters. Seek to understand the reasoning and dynamics underlying the three stages as explained.

Duration also plays a special role in this relationship as its measurement is a key factor when outsiders are judging the progression of the relation. Duration provides an objective measure of how "generically correct" things are going as far as a timeline is concerned.

Duration alone is not as important as the specific activities and needs of the Co-partners as they go through each stage, but it is a useful measure for discussion. If it goes outside the guidelines, then something is starting to be worthy of investigation as to why.

So, for the purposes of discussion, here are the three generic time periods associated with the three stages of the Boyfriend/'Girlfriend Relationship.

- Casual Dating: 0-90 Days to 6 months (Ch. 13-A)
- Committed Dating: 6 months - 2 years (Ch. 13-B)
- Engaged: 0-2 years (Ch. 13-C)

These time periods are not written in stone, but they are indicative of the generic periods of time for each stage. Each will be discussed and explained in its related section. The age, the social circumstances, along with the external circumstances of the Co-partners can cause these Durations to be of practically any elastic time period, but when discussing the generic stages, these are the numbers.

For Whom Do Boyfriend/Girlfriend Relationships Specifically Apply?

Two subgroups of society are primarily involved in seeking a companion of the opposite sex.

Teens and Twenties

For teens and twenties, there are many opportunities to meet similar age opposite sex dating partners through school events or other social events aimed at this age group. They have the means, the time, and the desire without really realizing it is as they go through their adolescence. It's just part of what's happening as they go about living their lives.

Once out of school, (employed or not) the built-in opportunities for social interaction begin to dwindle. Part of it may be that many in your social circle are already seriously dating or perhaps now your friends are getting married. If you aren't one of them then you may find yourself being gradually left behind.

Older Adults

For adults things become more problematic. If you are an older adult, perhaps newly divorced or widowed, then it's even more difficult as you have been "out of the scene" for so long, you may find it overwhelming to start "dating" again.

For the purpose of presenting a clear picture of the dynamics for these three stages of the Boyfriend/Girlfriend Relationships, I will be discussing them from the point of view of a younger member of society entering this arena for the first time. The elements of the "older dater" are complex and fraught with social customs.

From this point on I will endeavor to present a clear, middle of the road perspective from the point of view of the single Co-partner that is just entering the dating arena for the first time. But first, there is another possible topic involving the dating scene.

Are You Gay?

The question might come up, "If I am gay, how does *How Relationships Work* apply to me?" Up until now, the question of "gay or straight" hasn't been an issue. Nor is it much of a factor in the generic realties of the other eleven personal relationships (except perhaps Parent/Child from the birthing point of view.)

However, this could be a troublesome trait for you personally if you are (or think you might be) gay as far as maintaining acceptance from the outside straight world is concerned. If you are "out and proud" living in Sydney or San Francisco I'm not referring to you. This is more for the unknowingly gay or "possibly" gay person.

Given that the cultural, political, and political repercussions of being gay can be quite extreme depending on where you were born and how you were brought up; this is a serious question as to how all this "dating stuff" applies to you.

It's when you are first beginning to realize that you don't seem to have all the "hetero-feelings" that your same-sex friends are talking about, that you first become aware that you may be "different from the norm." There doesn't seem to be anyone else talking about the feelings *you* are experiencing, which is sexual attraction to your same sex.

As far as how these deeper dynamics work, I'm going to leave it up to the gay community to make their own decisions. You can decide for yourselves how HRW applies to your unique relationship dynamics. I suspect an entire subset of each of these three stages of "Boyfriend/Girlfriend" Relationship dynamics could be established in cooperation with input from the gay community. I look forward to this day.

When Courting Behavior Causes Trouble

Sexual flirting and attraction is completely normal and makes up an essential component of courting. Unfortunately, some of the sexual aspects of courting behavior can also become enmeshed in other human relationships which have nothing to do with sex. This causes trouble of various kinds.

First of all, most human societies have strong social taboos against sexual activity outside of the Husband/Wife Relationships, and this surprisingly often includes even the Boyfriend/Girlfriend relationships, again depending on the cultural, religious, and political customs of your birth. Also, sexual behavior is strongly forbidden within family relationships such as Parent/Child, Sibling/Sibling, or Grandparent/Grandchild Relationships in all human societies.

In general, strong taboos against courting behavior also exist in work, religious, and professional relationships. When Co-partners in relationships other than Boyfriend/Girlfriend or Husband/Wife become involved with the powerful dynamics of sexual attraction, this places an additional burden on their primary relationship. When this occurs, especially if it is based on a seduction, the damages can be substantial for the affected Co-partners, not to mention the Co-partners on the opposite sides of their primary seesaw relationships.

Again, for the purposes of discussion, what are presented in the next three chapters will be the ideal generic aspects of the Boyfriend/Girlfriend Relationships. There could be many instances in which Co-partners could violate community standards through their sexual dynamics. However, these next chapters are for the purpose of describing what would be healthy and normal dating attraction between willing and appropriate members of society consciously choosing the relationship. This has nothing at all to do with the aspect or dynamics of what are often termed "affairs."

The 90 Day Rule

Here is where I discuss one of the most important rules in all of *How Relationships Work.* Although this rule applies to all relationships, it has a special significance in the initial stages of the Boyfriend/Girlfriend interactions.

One reality of dating a new partner is that, no matter how much you like (or perhaps dislike) a person when first going out, it's going to take at least 90 days for your initial feelings to sort themselves out and to discover if something substantial is going to take their place.

This "90 Day Rule" is specifically designed to protect you during the "euphoric stage" of dating when the new person you have just started dating appears to be "The One" and you just can't stop thinking about how lucky you are and how wonderful your new dating partner is. This stage doesn't always occur in the beginning, but when it does its impact is very strong.

Potentially, there are thousands of positive "goo-goo" feelings you may have when first dating a new partner. The "90 Day Rule" states that you should not (must not) make any major decisions, nor even give the relationship any serious credence, until at least 90 days have passed.

This is a safety rule that protects you so that you don't get stung by a Co-partner who may or may not share your excitement. Your feelings may remain the same, but your Co-partner's feelings could change completely. Or, maybe you will be the Co-partner that all of a sudden changes his/her mind without warning. This rule is designed to protect you when all the wonderful things you thought you knew about your new Co-partner in the beginning, somehow start to evaporate right before your eyes.

The "90 Day Rule" also states that if, at the end of 90 days, your relationship is still strong (maybe even getting stronger) and both Co-partners want to increase their commitment, then you have passed a major milestone and have a basis for the next stage of dating which would be the committed or "going steady" stage. Probably less than 2 in 10 casual dating couples ever make it to the second stage.

So, if it's possible that you could benefit from this rule, it's here for you. This is something for you to know, and be aware of from your side of the seesaw while dating casually. However, be warned that this is not the exception, it is the rule, so be careful out there.

The Classic 90-Day Reversal

The way this typically works is that for the first 6 weeks you are extremely, possibly euphorically happy and feel "certain on the inside" that you have finally met your ideal mate for life. Then, sometime after six weeks goes by, some little chinks start to show up. Perhaps you find out that something first said to you actually isn't true. Or that the description of some place or situation doesn't quite meet the reality as it was described to you.

Then as reality rears its ugly head and more time goes by, you start seeing your new Co-partner for what he/she really is, and it may be a far cry from your original beliefs and feelings.

In fact, in the classic 90-Day Reversal, the exact reasons why you euphorically loved the person in the beginning now become the exact same reasons why you categorically hate this person now.

If this is something you've been through before, then you know what I'm talking about. If not, then you won't believe me anyway.

The Boyfriend/Girlfriend Relationship (Casual Dating)

Casual dating is the stage of dating any number of different partners with no major commitment. Each Co-partner is free to explore a variety of dating partners without pressure to make a commitment. During this stage, your Co-partner is considered your date. Calling a new dating partner a "boyfriend" or "girlfriend" is premature while casually dating.

In western culture, casual dating includes activities such as phone calls, flirtations, dances, dinners, drinks, parties, and holiday picnics. When Co-partners are in the casually dating stage, they may give less concern to future marriage partner issues. Typically they are young and just beginning to explore the wild journey of dating.

During this process of discovery, the dating partners compare and evaluate each other's age, social class, religion, height, weight, looks, education, intelligence, values, beliefs, goals, interests, and backgrounds. Each Co-partner makes independent decisions as to whether they wish to continue dating at a deeper level.

If all the comparisons are mutually favorable and the dating relationship lasts 3-6 months, the Casually Dating Relationship has a chance of moving to the nest courting stage.

Dating Partner/Dating Partner Environment (Casual Dating)

Courting must take place somewhere. It is important to keep in mind that, if the neurological attraction exists between two people, courting can take place in any environment. However, some Locations are designed specifically for courting while others are neutral or can even be hostile to courting activities. For "Casual Dating" the entire world is a stage. If you could just put all the singles together in one place and then only let them come out in pairs everything would go much easier.

❶ LOCATION

Single people typically go where other single people their age go so they can attract, meet, and interact with each other. Various Locations can satisfy this need for singles to make their selections and choices for courting activity.

For teens and twenties, there are:

- School social events
- Parties
- Bars
- Dance clubs
- Concerts

For older adults there are:

- Social events
- Health clubs
- Singles activities
- Video dating
- Newspaper ads

Depending on your circumstances you might be going out with groups of friends who are meeting other groups. You might be involved in some volunteer work, or club activities that naturally put you in the proximity of other singles.

❷ DURATION

Duration involves how long the Co-partners are together during each stage of the relationship. Duration is not expected for most Casual Dating Relationships. Here the Duration is perhaps meant to be short. Sort of like molecules bouncing around inside a nucleus.

For these dating experiences you might be meeting, going out for some brief interactions, and then deciding the person isn't what you are looking for. Its also part of the random aspect of attraction that living life can put you in many kinds of circumstance in which feeling attracted to another person was the last thing on your mind.

❸ TIMING

Timing in the Boyfriend/Girlfriend Relationships refers to the time of day that the Co-partners typically meet and interact. If they only see each other from 12:30 pm to 1:30 pm Saturday night, then this implies a different quality to the relationship than if the timing is every day for several hours in the afternoon and evening.

Typically when first dating, you need to find a convenient time when you can both get together during your busy schedules. Then you need to find some mutually agreeable activities. So, depending on circumstances, the initial Timing of your dating has a wide variety of "normal."

You may be attending a party with your group of friends, and make initial social contact. Or you could be scheduling a specific time and place for "a date." As far as the Timing goes, there are many experiences that could be called "times" that you dated or "went out" with a person. It's also part of this stage that even the definition of "a date" could be a point of contention.

Another aspect of Timing is that you may be involved with someone in another capacity. Perhaps you are both students, or you see each other in church group on Wednesday Nights. During this process of being laterally involved in non-dating activities, you find yourself developing feelings for the other person. This can happen before dating is an option or a topic of discussion.

Dating Partner/Dating Partner Structure (Casual Dating)

The Roles of the Boyfriend/Girlfriend Relationship are the attractive and desirable Male Role and the attractive and desirable Female Role. The superficial purpose behind each role is to present desirable attributes that attract the opposite sex.

Right there the future potential of this relationship depends on a subjective evaluation, not by you, but by your potential Co-partners. If you and 99 members of your gender were lined up in a row and ranked by "attractive and desirable" qualities, which number would you be?

This type of assessment is not being made by you but by members of the opposite sex, who only have their own selfish interests in mind to get the highest ranked choice possible. However, you are also part of group that is judging your opposite gender.

Much of these assessments occur below conscious awareness, and are heavily influenced by your social peers and the social milieu around where you live.

Compare and contrast the above assessments as might be made by the various dating Co-partners who live in: the USA, Russia, China, Iraq, India, South America, or perhaps Wellington, NSW. If you look exactly like Korea's most popular rock star, you might do well, unless you live in say in Bolivia.

Although it may not be contemplated consciously by the participants at the time, the bottom-line purpose of the Boyfriend/Girlfriend Relationship is to accumulate a wide set of experiences and guidelines for selecting a suitable partner for marriage. As such, the Dating Partner/Dating Partner Relationship is designed from the start to be an interim, not a permanent relationship.

❹ ROLES

Two roles are present: the single Male role and the single Female role.

Single Male

Be the guy who becomes involved with the girl in the physical activities of dating. Ideally this male would initiate the dating by asking the girl to a social event or at least be able to read the cues from the female indicating an invitation.

Single Male Role • Physical (Casually Dating)

Ideally, the Physical role of the Casually Dating Male is to:

- Take the girl out on dates
- Arrange transportation and pay for the date
- Not have expectations or pressure your date sexually
- Give small gifts or affectionate presents

Single Male Role • Emotional (Casually Dating)

Be the guy who becomes involved with the girl in the emotional activities of dating. Ideally, the Emotional role of the Casually Dating Male is to:

- Be nurturing and supportive
- Be attentive and respectful
- Be sincere about emotional feelings

Single Male Role • Mental (Casually Dating)

Be, the guy who becomes involved with the girl in the mental activities of dating. Ideally, the Mental role of the Casually Dating Male is to:

- Be interesting and interested during conversations
- Share non-threatening stories and anecdotes about self
- Be truthful and honest about thoughts and opinions
- Discuss interests and future goals

- Ask questions about your dating partner's opinions on different subjects

Single Male Role • Social (Casually Dating)

Be the guy who becomes involved with the girl in the social activities of dating. Ideally, the Social role of the Casually Dating Male is to:

- Bring date to fun and interesting social events
- Be respectful and considerate to dating partner, even if other girls or friends are present

Single Female

Be the girl who becomes involved with the guy in the emotional activities of dating.

Single Female Role • Physical (Casually Dating)

Ideally, the Physical role of the Casually Dating Female is to:

- Be prepared and ready when dating partner arrives

Single Female Role • Emotional (Casually Dating)

Be the girl who becomes involved with the guy in the emotional activities of dating. Ideally, the Emotional role of the Casually Dating Female is to:

- Be friendly and participate in date
- Be attentive and respectful to dating partner
- Be sincere about emotional feelings

Single Female Role • Mental (Casually Dating)

Be the girl who becomes involved with the guy in the mental activities of dating. Ideally, the Mental role of the Casually Dating Female is to:

- Be interesting and interested during conversations
- Share non-threatening stories and anecdotes about self

- Be truthful and honest about thoughts and opinions
- Discuss interests and future goals
- Ask questions about dating partner's thoughts on different subjects

Single Female Role • Social (Casually Dating)

Be the girl who becomes involved with the guy in the social activities of dating. Ideally, the Social role of the Casually Dating Female is to:

- Go with dating partner to fun and interesting social events
- Be respectful and considerate to dating partner, even if other boys or friends are present

❺ RULES

The Rules of the Boyfriend/Girlfriend Relationship are complex and interlaced with customs of many kinds. From this point on with the Boyfriend/Girlfriend Relationships I will list both the male and female sides as one dating Co-partner.

This is so the Reader can do his/her best to link and compare their understanding of dating to the following "generic" descriptions. Just pick the best logic of how it makes sense for you. And keep in mind, this section is about the structure of the relationship, not the Two Co-partners.

Dating Partner Rules • Physical (Casually Dating)

Physically, the Casually Dating Co-partners should:

- Be punctual
- Be polite
- Maintain eye contact with each other
- Address each other by their first name
- Not get overly involved
- Give each other "space"

- Discuss sexual activity and concerns (if appropriate)
- Dress appropriately for date

Dating Partner Rules • Emotional (Casually Dating)

Emotionally, the Casually Dating Co-partners should:

- Be sincere with their romantic interest
- Evaluate their Co-partner's romantic attraction to them
- Respect each other's privacy
- Not get overly involved
- Give each other emotional "space"
- Not complain or discuss dating details of previous Dating (or ex-Marriage) Co-partners
- Be wary of showing mutual trust
- Help the other Co-partner by contributing to the conversation
- Show positive signs and signals if they like the other person
- Not continue dating if they don't like the other person
- Not be a sexual tease unless they are serious
- Be open to (but not desperate for) a "love connection"

Dating Partner Rules • Mental (Casually Dating)

Mentally, the Casually Dating Co-partners should:

- Be more polite than truthful. (Andrew's rule)
- Keep shared confidences
- Discuss their goals and values
- Explore and discuss any mutual interests or hobbies
- Not tell a new romance any particulars of an old romance
- Discuss sexual activity and concerns

Dating Partner Rules • Social (Casually Dating)

Socially, the Casually Dating Co-partners should:

- Contact the other as soon as possible if going to be late or unable to attend a committed date
- Not criticize each other publicly
- Support the other person in his/her absence

❻ CUSTOMS

The Customs of the Boyfriend/Girlfriend Relationship (Casually Dating Co-partners edition) are completely dependent on the cultural, political, and religious customs of the dating partners.

Each human culture has a stage, sponsored and supported by that society's cultural standard, where dating activity is encouraged. If any of the cultural, religious and/or political backgrounds differ between the two Co-partners, special attention must be paid to validate and accommodate each other's differences.

Many courtship customs are social and religious in origin. Before the birth of the "true love" ideals in the fourteenth century, marriage was an economic and political event. Perhaps the best way to put it perhaps is that marriage could be a potentially non-working way for a family of making money or increasing social status.

So in this situation, the decision of potential unions between families was not up to the Co-partners, but rather was made by the adults with a vested interest in the economic union of the Two-Co-partners.

Dating Partner Customs • Cultural

Customs associated with the Boyfriend/Girlfriend Relationships of western are:

- Giving flowers or candy
- Males opening and holding doors for females

- Moonlight strolls
- Romantic dinners
- Holding hands in darkened theaters
- Walks along the beach
- Exchanging gifts

Dating Partner Customs • Religious

Certainly a religious custom might suggest that dating Co-partner would not have sexual relations until they were betrothed. Another might be that if you are planning to marry, it should be someone of the same religion.

Dating Partner Customs • Political

Politics is not something that typically enters into the Boy-friend/Girlfriend relationship. The couple is typically too much into each other to care about politics. Or, perhaps a couple met while pursing a similar set of political ideals agenda or career. Maybe they both were supporting the same candidate. As a result, their intimacy grew through the shared activities of promoting a third party.

Dating Partner/Dating Partner Co-partners (Casual Dating)

Young members of human societies begin courting behavior with the onset of puberty although courting behavior can take place between Co-partners at any age thereafter. During these modern times, more single, divorced, and widowed people than ever are exhibiting and participating in courtship behavior. Keep in mind however, that most courting behavior is being signaled below conscious or verbal awareness.

Many traits that measure attraction and various levels of interest have been presented by researchers and pollsters, who offer differing conclusions as to which traits are most truly generic. A wide disparity also exists between what people say they want and what they actually pursue or are willing to accept. These traits more typically might be considered under the Needs section of the individual Co-partners.

Each Co-partner is seeking a combination of the most desirable traits in his/her Co-partner. These Traits are based partly on current social fads and partly on biological imperatives. A distinction must he made, however, between personal Traits, such as an individual's physical appearance or intelligence, and the traits that facilitate participating in relationships.

From the HRW point of view, the seven Traits of HRW continue to determine how well each Co-partner will function in any relationship.

During the Casually Dating Relationships however a plethora of additional traits of a Co-partner are being evaluated. This combination, appreciation, and potential access to the other Co-partner's Traits are what keep the relationship potential alive.

Situations and events may conspire to contribute to relationships that aren't meant to go past the Casually Dating stage but are nonetheless valid experiences during this early stage of courting.

❼ TRAITS

The purpose of courtship is to compare the various traits between dating choices. However for the new Casually Dating Co-partner, "having fun" is typically the most pressing issue. As a younger person in society you are biologically compelled to engage in human procreation generically speaking. Whether and how you follow through with these actions is a personal choice each individual makes for him/her self.

Dating Partner Traits • Being Attracted (Casual Dating)

The Boyfriend/Girlfriend Relationship classically begins with the single Trait of physical attraction between Co-partners. The nature of this attraction features a confluence of fascination and exclusivity, combined with sexual desire. This distinct state of chemistry is so strong and so visceral that it can motivate behavior to extremes. It is mission-critical that this attraction be present on some level for two people to continue dating and in order to advance to the second stage of courtship.

Know that much of this attraction takes place on a non-verbal level. Sexual interest is often triggered by signals such as extended gaze, pupil dilation, touching, and body postures. This type of physical communication, which takes place below conscious awareness, signals a high level of interest for the other person. These signs may or may not be noticed by the person experiencing them, but this body language can easily be read by others.

Dating Partner Traits • Being Committed (Casual Dating)

When first dating Being Committed means that you both get home alive and in one piece as your "commitment" only extends to the end of the date. In fact being committed past that point is inappropriate in that it may or may not have any meaning or relevance for your Co-partner.

This Trait is developed during the exploratory phase of casual dating. By definition you are not committed until you know your dating partner enough to want to explore this option. If the Co-partners are sufficiently similar in a number of important criteria, they will begin to desire commitment. If they develop a sense of security and belonging that continues to sustain interest, they will be motivated to stay on the dating relationship seesaw.

Dating Partner Traits • Being Genuine (Casual Dating)

Being Genuine during the Casual Dating stage is hard to come by. In theory you would want to hold back your deepest feelings certainly, but it would also be nice to be truthful in the more superficial areas of conversation.

Most dating partners are eager to put themselves in the best possible light so there is much "presentation" between the Two Co-partners. In a flash a Co-partner might exaggerate his/her resources either knowingly or unknowingly. Or perhaps he/she downplays a negative topic and steers the conversation in another direction. If we are too happy dating this person we might not notice some of these suspect behaviors. For now, we're just glad to be dating at all. A substantial amount of time is spent on grooming and preparing for dates which is unlikely to last as the relationship progresses.

Dating Partner Traits • Being Trustworthy (Casual Dating)

Being Trustworthy is a Trait that Co-partners begin to look for as the relationship becomes more serious. For now, who cares about that? Maybe the least trustworthy person is the most exciting and attracts all the attention from the opposite sex. Does this person keep his/her word? "Who cares? Where's the Party!" Is he/she dependable? Answer, "I don't know, let's find out."

It's during this casual stage of dating that you will learn what traits are and how they apply as you are making arrangements to go out together. If you are trying to change your "persona" it will take a lot of effort to maintain the impressions that you want to make on the other person. If you are never going to see the person again who cares? But if this person is going to become your future steady dating partner, you will be found out.

Does what your dating Co-partner say, correspond with what your dating Co-partner does? Incidents of trustworthiness (or lack thereof) begin to accumulate and are noted by both Co-partners with an eye towards the future. One problem is these early clues tend to be missed or ignored during the first few months of a new romance. You might be forced to compromise your original expectations. If he/she doesn't call back as soon as you'd like, is that because you are being too needy or because he/she doesn't care? This may take weeks, maybe months to determine.

Dating Partner Traits • Being Emotionally Mature (Casual Dating)

If the Co-partners are of young or similar age, then Being Emotionally Mature could be last on their list of concerns. Yet this Trait might be carefully evaluated by the older Co-partner looking ahead to marriage. This Trait defines that a person is emotionally and mentally prepared to take on the long-term commitment that marriage represents.

So here would be a good time to say that thinking of future marriage partners when first casually dating is not a winning strategy. A better strategy would be to get to know the person you are with and see if you like them or not. If you are prescreening all of your prospective dating partners for marriage potential, you will have far fewer experiences to test.

In various cultures there are many considerations that factor into the concept of maturity. Do the Co-partners have financial support? Does either Co-partner have to finish school? Are they making mature evaluations of their future based on their current activities?

For the "Casually Dating" Co-partners there's no set agenda, no final destination. There's today and maybe the weekend. If both Co-partners are single and interested then who's to say what they do with each other on their own time. They could be two unlikely Co-partners making the best of a bad situation. They could be the alpha male/female of the pack. Once a dating couple pair-off, they create their own world.

Dating Partner Traits • Having Communication Skills (Casual Dating)

Do you "speak each other's language" Do you feel that this person can complete your sentences? Can you talk and share what for you are intimate disclosures for hours in meaningful ways with little effort? The special communication that new dating couples share is often the biggest clue to their attraction.

Perhaps one of the Co-partners is very good at making the other feel at ease. He/she makes the awkwardness go away by their easy natural style. But latter, the communication skills that made things easy in the beginning, might become indicative of a shallow and superficial personality with nothing deeper to say. Who knew?

Dating Partner Traits • Having Problem-Solving Skills (Casual Dating)

"Problems? _____ and I could never have any problems." This might be how your dating relationship begins, but this stage won't last long.

Having Problem-solving Skills will be well-tested during the Boyfriend/Girlfriend Relationship. During each stage of courtship, problems and conflicts give both Co-partners ample opportunity to practice conflict resolution skills. Ideally, a positive pattern of mutual problem-solving and conflict resolution will be established during the Boyfriend/Girlfriend Relationship.

Casual Dating could be so brief that problems never enter your dating interactions. Or it might be turn out that no matter what you do with _____, there's always a catastrophic problem to deal with. It's only by casually dating that you would ever find this out.

❽ NEEDS

The Casually Dating (and Committed Dating Co-partners) may be meeting personal needs within the Boyfriend/Girlfriend Relationship that take precedence over future long-term concerns such as marriage.

Here we are going to list the Needs of the Boyfriend/Girlfriend Relationship that each gender seeks in a Co-partner from either male or female perspective.

Dating Partner Needs • Physical (Casual Dating)

Physically, each Co-partner has a need for:

- A member of the opposite sex to go out with
- Nonsexual physical contact
- An outlet for sexual expression whether real or feigned

Physically, each Co-partner needs (is looking for) a dating partner who matches his/her expectations and/or desires as far as:

- Height
- Weight
- Beauty
- Health
- Age
- Sex appeal
- Athletic ability
- Being attracted to him/her

Dating Partner Needs • Emotional (Casual Dating)

Emotionally, each Co-partner needs a dating partner who is looking for:

- Someone of the opposite sex to love and share themselves with
- A member of the opposite sex to love and accept them
- Is attracted to them emotionally
- Is someone he/he can get along with
- Has a positive personality
- Likes him/her romantically
- Will treat him/her in a positive manner
- Is sensitive to his/her feelings

Dating Partner Needs • Mental (Casual Dating)

Mentally, each Co-partner has a need for:

- Stimulation and excitement
- Entertainment

Mentally, each Co-partner wants a dating partner who matches his/her expectations and/or desires as far as:

- Education
- Intelligence
- Values
- Beliefs
- Goals
- Interests
- Having a personality
- Being interesting to talk to
- Having demonstrated achievement
- Shows common sense
- Having a good sense of humor
- Is rational and not too emotional

Dating Partner Needs • Social(Casual Dating)

Socially, each Co-partner has a need for:

- A date to go to social functions
- A date who will impress and build status with his/her social peers

Socially, each Co-partner wants a dating partner who

- Matches his/her expectations and/or desires as far as:
- Social background and/or class
- Race
- Religion
- Political background

❾ TACTICS

Courtship tactics take on legendary proportion. During the beginning stages of courtship, there is a high amount of positive self-presentation (putting self in best possible light).

Here is where the saying, "All is fair in love and war" lives. Another tactic would be working strategically towards a win/win with your Co-partner in a Boyfriend/Girlfriend Relationship. However, if you are the only one doing this the relationship may still not be successful and it will have nothing to do with you.

Single Male Tactics

Here are some suggestions of tactics as coming from both sides of the Casually Dating Relationship.

Male Tactics • Positive (Casual Dating)

Some typically Positive Tactics are:

- Sending flowers
- Writing romantic poetry
- Giving small yet meaningful gifts

Male Tactics • Negative (Casual Dating)

Some typically Negative Tactics to watch out for are:

- Lying about sincerity of affection
- Making unannounced visits
- Assuming plans without checking
- Giving false or insincere compliments
- Not liking fat
- Judging a girl by her breasts, hair, or other bodily parts
- Trying to keep a relationship going against the wishes of the other Co-partner
- Giving expensive gifts to buy affection

Single Female Tactics

Female Tactics • Positive (Casual Dating)

Some typically Positive Tactics to watch out for are:

- Asking questions to stimulate conversations
- Sharing some non-threatening opinions
- Not engaging in verbal foreplay
- Being yourself

Female Tactics • Negative (Casual Dating)

Some Negative Female Tactics:

- Judging a guy by his height, buns, shoulders, or stomach
- Going for a famous jock
- Dating someone just because he has money
- Trying to keep a relationship going against the wishes of the other Co-partner
- Playing sexual games to attract attention

*T*he Boyfriend/Girlfriend Relationship (Committed Dating)

By now the Casually Dating couple has been out enough times, and had enough experiences with each other, to pass a fairly rigorous set of standards. Through a process of discovery and interaction they have formally agreed to become a committed couple. From this point forward, they are considered Boyfriend and Girlfriend and start becoming known to others as a couple.

The couple has been out together now a number of times with social groups, parties, and other group activities. Now there's more desire for "alone time" so that they can be together. They are happy just to be alone to communicate and share directly with each other without outside interruptions. Depending on their external circumstances and country of origin this could be anywhere from easy to next to impossible.

Boyfriend/Girlfriend Environment (Committed Dating)

❶ LOCATION

Now that they don't have the pressure to "meet someone" the couple can share more personal time directly with each other. Depending on their circumstances, this might include intimate dinners with just them, picnics where they are alone, or any environment where they can simply be with each other and not be disturbed.

The couple doesn't have to have the most exciting "single atmospheres" to go out, because being together is already better than being alone in a more highly charged dating atmosphere. They will probably schedule their dating choices to fit in with their social group although this group will know them to be a couple.

❷ DURATION

The assumption is that they have dated casually for enough time to like each other and become committed. Typically this takes at least 3 - 6 months. The start of this second stage of their Boyfriend/Girlfriend relation is marked by the day they declare to their social group they have formalized their commitment by announcing they are "going steady" or have exchanged meaningful tokens of their commitment.

❸ TIMING

They should now have some regular and committed times they see each other depending on their schedule. What they are going to do is not as important as that they are going to be together. They can relax with the knowledge that on Friday night, or New Years Eve they will be together. They might have a choice of going to a wild party or staying home and watching a DVD/video.

Boyfriend/Girlfriend Structure (Committed Dating)

Committed dating leaves the stressful world of dating many partners to the mutual commitment of dating only one partner. During this stage, your Co-partner is considered your boyfriend or girlfriend. The initial criterion of physical attraction and superficial traits now takes secondary importance to the emotional, mental, and social concerns of the other person's traits and personality.

As the Two Co-partners continue Committed Dating, they begin to view themselves increasingly as a couple. They spend more time with each other in a wider range of activities and settings. They begin a mutual disclosure of interests and personal aspects of each other's lives. Friends and family now become a major influence on the Committed dating couple.

During this stage, the Co-partners are more likely to express interest in each other's daily activities, depend upon each other for personal counsel, get angry in front of each other, and be sexually faithful. There is an increase in love, but there is also an increase in the level of emotional investment.

Much of the Co-partners dating activities will necessarily revolve around the current activities and lifestyle of the Co-partners. If they are both in high school or college for example, this will rule their outer world. If they are both working, then that implies another set of circumstances.

❹ ROLES

Boyfriend Role

Be the guy who becomes involved with the girl in the physical activities of dating.

Boyfriend Role • Physical

Ideally, the Physical role of the Boyfriend is to:

- Continue as before with your girlfriend, plus
- Engage in physically affectionate behavior

Boyfriend Role • Emotional

Ideally, the Emotional role of the Boyfriend is to become involved with the girlfriend in the emotional activities of dating.

- Be emotionally ready and desirous of a committed dating relationship
- Share deeper feelings with girlfriend about what's important to you
- Always consider the affects of your plans on your girlfriend
- Discuss future plans and dating activities
- Reveal deeper feelings as relationship progresses
- Share hopes, dreams, future plans

Boyfriend Role • Mental

Be, the Boyfriend involved in the mental activities of dating. Ideally, the Mental role of the Committed Dating Male is to:

- Explore your Co-partner's likes and dislikes through activities
- Discuss plans for the future as it would affect his Co-partner

Boyfriend Role • Social

Be the Boyfriend who is involved with the girlfriend in the social activities of dating.

- Always consider the affects of your plans on your girlfriend
- Discuss future plans and dating activities
- Bring girlfriend to family events, holidays, and celebrations

Girlfriend Role

Girlfriend Role • Physical

Be the Girlfriend who becomes involved with the guy in the physical activities of dating.

Girlfriend Role • Emotional

Ideally, the Emotional role of the Girlfriend is to:

- Be emotionally ready and desirous of a committed dating relationship
- Share deeper feelings with boyfriend about what's important to you
- Not subjugate self to make things go smoother

Girlfriend Role • Mental

Be the Girlfriend who becomes involved with the guy in the mental activities of dating.

- Share thoughts and feelings on future goals
- Defend your opinions on various topics of conversation
- Don't pretend to be dumber or smarter than you are

Girlfriend Role • Social

Be the Girlfriend who becomes involved in the social activities of dating. Ideally, the Social role of the Committed Dating Female is to:

- Always consider the affects of your plans on boyfriend
- Discuss future plans and dating activities
- Bring boyfriend to family events, holidays, and celebrations

❺ RULES

Again, the age of the Co-partners, where they live, the family environment, if they are in school, and many other factors all become intertwined as the Co-partners continue to go out with each other.

Boyfriend/Girlfriend Rules • Physical

Physically, the Committed Dating Co-partners should:

- Be dating each other exclusively

Boyfriend/Girlfriend Rules • Emotional

Emotionally, the Committed Dating Co-partners should:

- Show interest in each other's daily activities
- See each other regularly
- Support each other emotionally
- Share news of success
- Celebrate birthdays and important holidays together
- Not be socializing or living with old boyfriends/girlfriends

Boyfriend/Girlfriend Rules • Mental

Mentally, the Committed Dating Co-partners should:

- Be tolerant of each other's same sex friends
- Be completely honest about their needs
- Involve themselves in mutually enjoyable activities
- Be wary of moving in or living together
- Could begin some light discussion on marriage topic

Boyfriend/Girlfriend Rules • Social

Socially, the Committed Dating Co-partners should:

- Let other people know they are a couple
- Introduce each other to important family and social relationships
- Attend social functions together as a couple

❻ CUSTOMS

The Customs of the Boyfriend/Girlfriend Relationship are completely dependent on the cultural, political, and religious customs of the couple. If the cultural, political, and religious backgrounds differ for the two Co-partners, special attention should be paid to validate and accommodate each other's differences.

Boyfriend/Girlfriend Customs • Cultural

Customs associated with the committed Boyfriend/Girlfriend Relationships are:

- – Meeting the parents
- – Visiting each others homes
- – Attending family events as a couple

Boyfriend/Girlfriend Customs • Political

If either of the Co-partners is particularly political, then this could become an aspect of the relationship.

Boyfriend/Girlfriend Customs • Religious

Religion may not be a particularly important aspect for one or both of the Co-partners. But, if they are not from the same (or similar enough) religion then this factor could become increasingly important.

Boyfriend/Girlfriend Co-partners (Committed Dating)

The Co-partners like each other, and now are going to be spending more time, both intimate and social time with each other's families. Their defenses will have dropped for the most part, so now will come some opportunities for seeing the Co-partner in more typical day-to-day activities where the deeper aspects of the HRW traits will be exposed.

❼ TRAITS

The first tests of the various traits to seek in a Dating Co-partner have been made. However, there is now another series of questions being asked by both Co-partners, whether consciously or unconsciously, as to the suitability of the other for a long-term commitment.

Depending on how long they have been dating exclusively and their ages, etc, each Co-partner will still be comparing their Co-partner combination of desirable traits against which may start including some non-desirable traits. For example, Billy might be the nicest guy on earth, until he has a few drinks and starts punching everybody. Or Lisa may be so cute and perky, but she's throwing up her dinner every night and you've just found out about it because her best friend told you.

Boyfriend/Girlfriend Traits • Being Attracted

Are you finding out things about your Co-partner that make you feel even more proud that you are dating? Does it seem that she's even prettier without her make-up, or is the thought of her without make-up a bit scary? Have you seen your healthy fit athletically superior boyfriend living on pizza and ice cream? Is that car you really liked that person for just on loan?

If you liked someone for one or two reasons that sealed the deal for you, are those things now more in the background as you get to know more about this person you are going steady with?

Boyfriend/Girlfriend Traits • Being Committed

Dating exclusively is a lot harder than it looks. As you gaze around at the other singles in your life, do you imagine that they having more fun than you or are you smugly happy that you aren't one of them. Is there another (boy/girl) that has caught your eye? Are you wondering what dating him/her might be like?

Perhaps your "exclusive partner" was the flirt of his/her social group. Has that person stopped such behavior or is he/she acting like they are still single, especially when you are not around? And when you bring it up, are you accused of being jealous or insecure? Now you have to ask yourself more deeply if you are happy to remain committed to one dating partner and if your Co-partner is doing the same.

Boyfriend/Girlfriend Traits • Being Genuine

Whatever pretense or manufactured qualities you presented before are now going to be fading away. Perhaps what looked so good now looks even better. Before you weren't sure that your Co-partner was a nice person, but now you are certain because you've seen so many examples of this in the "real world." Perhaps what you saw as a natural beauty is really the result of an hour of preparation time.

Once you are dating exclusively you will have multiple opportunities to find out what is "really real" about your Co-partner, and what isn't. Pay attention as what you are learning now may become supremely important as time goes by.

Boyfriend/Girlfriend Traits • Being Trustworthy

Is your Co-partner trustworthy? Does he/she do what he/she says? Are they good with you but try to cheat others? Does he/she pretend to be religious (because you are) but you can now tell that they don't have a religious bone in their body? As the days go by, the experiences will accumulate and you and your Co-partner will both be "building a case" as to how trustworthy you are in various situations.

Boyfriend/Girlfriend Traits • Being Emotionally Mature

Depending on the age of the Co-partners, emotionally maturity may not be high on the list for you or your Co-partner. However, it's a good sign if your Co-partner does seem mature, and able to handle day-to-day stressors in a way you find admirable as opposed to embarrassing.

Boyfriend/Girlfriend Traits • Having Communication Skills

With Co-partners who are dating exclusively, you might expect that they have an easy going, shared communication style that seems to match both personalities. Is this true in your case, or is one of you the wild screamer when things don't go his/her way? Is your Co-partner good at communicating his/her true feelings? Are you?

Having Communication Skills is a Trait that is tested through-out courtship. In fact, no other relationship has the dramatic range of dynamics as when two complete strangers meet and go through the courting stages to become husband and wife.

As couples spend increasing time alone, they have many opportunities to share their thoughts, feelings, and needs with each other. A significant portion of their communication should be directed towards the nature of their relationship and how they feel about its progress.

Boyfriend/Girlfriend Traits • Having Problem-Solving Skills

During exclusive dating you will certainly experience problems and conflicts that arise. These might be problems that the two of you create for each other, or problems that you have to deal with as an individual or couple from outside sources.

This positive trait is hard to find in any person, much less a dating Co-partner, so it would be valuable to make note of how your Co-partner resolves problems, especially as they reflect you as a couple. This will portend how problems are dealt with in the future when the stakes could be much higher.

❽ NEEDS

Prior to getting married, the Casually Dating and Committed Dating Co-partners may be meeting personal needs within the Boyfriend/Girlfriend Relationship that take precedence over future thoughts of marriage.

The quest to meet each Co-partner's needs in the Boyfriend/Girlfriend Relationship is complicated by the following considerations:

1) As a single person, each Co-partner has personal needs he/she would like to be fulfilled
2) Each Co-partner is looking for specific qualities in the other person
3). Each Co-partner is bartering what they have for what the other person might have

Boyfriend/Girlfriend Needs

As you mature in your relationship, you will find your needs changing as your lifestyle changes. You are now dating exclusively, this can change your needs right there.

Boyfriend/Girlfriend Needs • Physical

Physically, each Co-partner has a need for:

- One person to commit as a dating partner
- A romantic relationship on which he/she can depend

Boyfriend/Girlfriend Needs • Emotional

Emotionally, each Co-partner has a need to:

- Feel a sense of commitment
- Have someone he/she can depend on
- Get along with someone who likes him/her romantically

Emotionally, each dating Co-partner needs a Co-partner who is:

- Caring
- Affectionate
- Considerate
- Emotionally sensitive
- Can accept his/her negatives as well as positives

Boyfriend/Girlfriend Needs • Mental

Mentally, each Co-partner needs a Committed Dating Partner who will:

- Treat him/her with respect
- Be someone he/she can trust and
- Understood him/her
- Support him/her

Mentally, each Co-partner wants a Committed Dating Partner who:

- Is intelligent
- Has demonstrated achievement
- Shares similar interests
- Shows common sense
- Is a good conversationalist
- Has a good sense of humor
- Is someone he/she can talk to
- Is someone he/she can depend on

Mentally, each Co-partner needs someone who will:

- Treat him/her with respect
- Be someone he/she can trust and depend to understand
- Support him/her if the going gets rough

Mentally, each Co-partner wants a person who:

- Is intelligent
- Has demonstrated achievement
- Shares similar interests
- Shows common sense
- Is a good conversationalist
- Has a good sense of humor
- Is someone he/she can talk to

Boyfriend/Girlfriend Needs • Social

Socially, each Co-partner has a need to:

- Show others he/she is worthy

Socially, each Co-partner wants a person who:

- Is acceptable to his/his family
- Is acceptable to his/her race
- Has similar religious beliefs
- Is fun to be with in a group of people
- Likes the same activities he/she does
- Won't embarrass him/her socially

❾ TACTICS

Ultimately, the overall need of the courting Co-partner is to find a mate for marriage. The goal is to find the best possible person with whom to share a life and build a family. But this overall priority doesn't really come to the fore until such time as the Co-partner is seeking a marriage partner

Prior to getting married, the Casually Dating and Committed Dating Co-partners may be meeting personal needs within the Boyfriend/Girlfriend Relationship that take precedence over future thoughts of marriage.

Boyfriend/Girlfriend Tactics

Tactics should now be geared towards "getting along" and being comfortable with each other. As your relationship progresses, you will feel subtle pulls and various manipulations, both within the relationship and from others.

There's a good chance that the strategies and tactics you used within your family dynamics, with parents and/or siblings for example, will be displayed and tested in your current Boyfriend/Girlfriend relationship.

Boyfriend/Girlfriend Tactics • Positive

Some typically Positive Tactics are:

- Giving special birthday and anniversary gifts
- Keeping communication true and honest
- Nipping problems in the bud
- Learning when to give in and when to stand firm
- (if older) Paying for the baby sitter will earn big points

Boyfriend/Girlfriend Tactics • Negative

Some typically Negative Tactics to watch out for are:

- Flirting with or dating other Co-partners
- Playing psychological games to gain advantage
- Pursing personal agendas that are counter to the goals of the relationship
- Withholding secrets or important information
- Pretending or hoping problems will fix themselves.

CHAPTER 13-C

The Boyfriend/Girlfriend Relationship (Engaged Dating)

The Boyfriend/Girlfriend Co-partners have now taken their biggest step yet of becoming engaged. Perhaps they did this through a well thought out, genuine, and mature progression with caution and some detours along the way. Or perhaps they've just met and thought it would be funny if they "got engaged" just to freak out their friends. Assuming it's the former; both Co-partners are now happy and feel certain that getting married is the next step for them.

Whatever the situation, once a couple is engaged, it becomes the right and some would say even the duty, of family members, friends, and associated economic, religious, and governmental organizations to become involved and start sharing their 2 cents of how and what the couple should be doing with their lives.

Make no mistake, once you become engaged, you are no longer "a couple" but are a future part of a culture with a religious and political agenda, which as an upstanding members of this society, you are expected to be. The focus is no longer on you as the couple, and what you want, it's now about what everybody else wants from you as a couple.

Depending on how and when you announced your intention to wed, you will begin, as a couple, to receive an amazing amount of input about what you should and should not do, and your feelings as that couple, aren't always part of this discussion.

Now the story of the proposal becomes the mandatory and oft repeated tale. Whether to have an "engagement party" or not may not even be up to the couple anymore. Once engaged, it seems that society has only one objective in mind and that is the wedding and when is it going to take place?

Fiancé/Fiancée Environment (Engaged Dating)

Depending on your situation and future plans, there is a wide range of potential Environments that you could find yourself in.

❶ LOCATION

You are a couple now. People have expectations. When you are invited somewhere it may be assumed that you are to bring your future spouse. Life may continue on as before, but your future marriage will be on many people's minds. Perhaps you've both graduated from college now and must decide where you are going to live. You might want to move in together and see how that goes.

❷ DURATION

The moment you are engaged, the clock starts ticking to your nuptials. If you are still in school, people will wait until you graduate. If you remain engaged over two years without getting married people will begin to doubt your intentions. A Duration of between 6 months to 2 years is considered generically acceptable for your engagement period. Being Engaged for longer than 2 years becomes suspect unless there is a significant reason that everyone understands.

❸ TIMING

Now as opposed to spending time with just your Co-partner in peace, you are *always* going to be going out on Fridays or Sundays *have to* be spent at the parents. You may find yourselves spending a lot more time together than before, but interacting more with the other Co-partner's family or social milieu so they can check out who their son/daughter is marrying. You may be getting the sense that your life is not actually your own as you were expecting it to be.

Fiancé/Fiancée Structure
(Engaged Dating)

Engagement is a formal commitment by the Co-partners and is recognized by their society as an intention to get married. This is the final stage of courtship. Both parties feel secure as to the future of their relationship and they begin mutual arrangements in preparation for a Husband/Wife Relationship.

During this stage many diverse situations can occur that will test the strength of the future marriage as well as lay the groundwork for your future experience of the dreaded In-law/In-law Relationships.

Planning the wedding is just one involved experience that can bring up many issues for all concerned. Many opportunities are typically presented for the engaged couple to discuss their future lives together with their future in-laws. Of the many Boyfriend/Girlfriend Relationships initiated, perhaps less than one percent actually continues through all three stages.

❹ ROLES

Two roles are present: the man who is engaged to be married is called his partner's fiancé and the woman is called her partner's fiancée.

Fiancé (Male)

Be the Fiancé who becomes involved with the girl in the physical activities of preparing for marriage.

Fiancé (Male) Physical Role

Ideally, the Physical role of the Fiancé is to:

- Continue with you prior activities with your fiancée
- Give a symbol of engagement to the betrothed
- Get blood tests, medical examinations, etc

Fiancé (Male) Emotional Role

Ideally, the Emotional role of the Engaged Male is to:

- Be emotionally ready and desirous of the marriage relationship
- Give deep thought to your future plans and what it all means

Fiancé (Male) Mental Role

Typically, the Mental role of the Engaged Male is to:

- Discuss and put into action the wedding preparation
- Be aware of and considerate to social future wife's expectations
- Discuss expectations of marriage and role of marriage partner
- Bring up and resolve any reservations or hesitations on your part before getting married
- Bring up the "children" question and see how that goes

Fiancé (Male) Social Role

Be the Fiancé who becomes involved with the girl in the social activities of dating. Ideally, the Social role of the Engaged Male is to:

- Meet with and get to know the future in-laws
- Bring your Fiancée home to meet the family
- Have a financial plan in place
- Fill out paperwork
- Choose the ceremony celebrant, etc

Fiancée (Female)

Fiancée (Female) Physical Role

Ideally, the Physical role of the Fiancée is to:

- Continue your prior activities with your fiancé
- Receive a symbol of engagement to the betrothed
- Get blood tests, medical examinations, etc

Fiancée (Female) Emotional Role

Ideally, the Emotional role of the Engaged Female is to:

- Be emotionally ready and desirous of the marriage relationship
- Discuss expectations of marriage and role of marriage partner
- Discuss the concept of children, when and how many

Fiancée (Female) Mental Role

Ideally, the Mental role of the Engaged Female is to:

- Discuss and put into action the preparation for wedding
- Be aware of and considerate to future Husband's desires for wedding
- Bring up and resolve any reservations or hesitations on your part before getting married
- Oversee wedding preparations

Fiancée (Female) Social Role

Ideally, the Social role of the Engaged Female is to:

- Meet with and get to know the future in-laws
- File paperwork
- Meet and deal with all the people and decisions that a wedding involves

❺ RULES

The Rules of the Boyfriend/Girlfriend Relationship are complex and interlaced with customs of all kinds. Many courtship customs are social and religious in origin.

Fiancé/Fiancée Rules • Physical

Physically, the Engaged Co-partners should:

- Be dating each other exclusively
- Discuss sexual activity and concerns
- Provide each other with a symbol of their engagement
- Discuss medical conditions
- Fulfill obligations and paperwork, such as marriage license and blood tests

Fiancé/Fiancée Rules • Emotional

Emotionally, the Engaged Co-partners should:

- Discuss everything and anything prior to getting married
- Discuss future roles and expectations as husband and wife
- Be listening to Inner Conversations concerning marriage
- Be expecting some last minute jitters before wedding
- Cancel the wedding if in severe doubt about getting married or you have reservations about the person you are marrying (even if at the ceremony)

Fiancé/Fiancée Rules • Mental

Mentally, the Engaged Co-partners should:

- Discuss and mutually agree on wedding plans as much as possible
- Be communicating their thoughts, feelings, and needs to each other
- Be expecting outside interests to be put pressure on the union
- Discuss future goals and life expectations

- Discuss future living arrangements
- Discuss expectations for having children
- Discuss, analyze, and plan their financial future thoroughly
- Discuss what is desired or expected of each other as a spouse

Fiancé/Fiancée Rules • Social

Socially, the Engaged Co-partners should:

- Announce the engagement to family and friends
- Meet and get to know each other's parents and family as much as possible
- Plan and organize the wedding based on cultural background and expectations
- Discuss customs and rituals, especially if they differ

❻ CUSTOMS

The Customs of the Fiancé/Fiancée Relationship are completely dependent on the cultural, religious, and political customs of the betrothed. If these backgrounds differ for the two Co-partners, special attention should be paid to validate and accommodate each other's differences.

The more these potential problems can be identified and discussed the better. Couples "in love" are not always thinking about the consequences of their union as far as their respective family's are concerned.

Fiancé/Fiancée Customs • Cultural

Once you are engaged, you may experience some semi-support from your cultural society, in case you didn't have it before. If your Dating Co-partner wasn't particularly appreciated by your family, perhaps they might be more favorably disposed once you become engaged. Or maybe your dating history with your Co-partner has been a secret from your family because you were going to school in Indiana. Now you are bringing your Co-partner home for Thanksgiving to meet the parents.

Whatever your circumstances, becoming engaged is a secret you no longer want to keep, or if you do, then you know it's going to be a problem with one or both sets of parents.

Issues that may not have been of concern before could now come to the forefront such as age, income, color of your skin, future job prospects, and the list goes on. If you and your new betrothed have been dating under the radar of your family's cultural background you can be sure that these issues will quickly become front and center.

Fiancé/Fiancée Customs • Religious

Marriage is often sanctified by a religious ceremony chosen by the Co-partners. Marriage is certainly a political event as well, since it is a legal status that is monitored by governments. If there is a disparity in your religious beliefs, this is when it's going to start to rear its ugly head. Even if neither Co-partner is a particularly fervent religious practitioner, now is when the problems will start to arise from other family members who are.

Let's just pick a simple Catholic/Jewish combination of Engaged Co-partners. Are they getting married in a Catholic Church or a Jewish Synagogue? Is there such thing as a combined ceremony? What are the children who aren't even born yet going to be? Which family would be the most upset if the ceremony didn't go the way they want? Who's paying? Where's it going to be? Who has to travel? What were you thinking? If you were a Jewish/Moslem couple living in the Middle East how much more intense would these conversations become?

Fiancé/Fiancée Customs • Political

Politically speaking, possibly the biggest factor for the Engaged Couple might be the legality of their intended marriage. Perhaps they were thinking of getting married in Tahiti, but the French have some specific conditions that you weren't aware of before. Or perhaps a simple justice of the peace wedding won't fit the agenda of the politically connected In-laws. If an issue comes up, and it's a political football, then this is where it fits in the HRW assessment.

Fiancé/Fiancée Co-partners (Engaged Dating)

❼ TRAITS

Fiancé/Fiancée Traits • Being Attracted

The Fiancé/Fiancée better be attracted to each other, because here is where the pressure it going to start testing their attraction. Are they both willing and wanting each other enough to go through the ordeal of planning a wedding? If the proper time has passed and the couple feels strongly, there will still be many tests and situations that come up.

This is usually the time when the "old boyfriend/girlfriend" shows up and realizes the mistake they made breaking up with you (or your Co-partner). It's the one he/she always reminisced about.

Perhaps a newer, better, lusher potential Co-partner appears who specifically wants to save you from the "biggest mistake you are ever going to make." And, what's strange is that everything that's missing with your current Co-partner is fulfilled completely by the promise of the new one. These choices will be yours to consider.

Fiancé/Fiancée Traits • Being Committed

Getting married is "the big one." Living with someone for the rest of your life, until "death do you part" pretty much defines Being Committed. Again, life has a funny way of testing you and your commitment, so hang on as the tests are being presented.

Sometimes just the fear of the unknown is enough to give either or both Co-partners "cold feet" so how you deal with this will be an excellent test of your commitment to each other and your future together.

Fiancé/Fiancée Traits • Being Genuine

During Casual and even Committed Dating the trait of Being Genuine is hard to come by but by now you better be revealing who you are and what you are about. If you have any deep dark secrets this is the time to reveal them. Although it may seem hard, if you are not Being Genuine for fear that your Co-partner won't marry you, how will he or she feel if you wait until you are married to share this information? How would your Co-partner feel if he/she were to learn this "secret" from another source?

Fiancé/Fiancée Traits • Being Trustworthy

Being Trustworthy is the Trait that says that everything you have said and done with your Co-partners up till now has been the truth, the whole truth, and nothing but the truth.

You have had ample time to judge and be judged. Do you keep your word? Has your Co-partner been dependable? You want to be able to rely on this trait of your Co-partner Being Trustworthy for the rest of your life. If you have your doubts, this is the time to bring them forward.

Fiancé/Fiancée Traits • Being Emotionally Mature

However Emotionally Mature you or your Co-partner may be, you will certainly be more so after a couple of years of marriage. The decisions you make now could impact future generations, so it would behoove both Co-partners to dig deep to determine if going forward with this marriage is the right thing to do.

Fiancé/Fiancée Traits • Having Communication Skills

Having Communication Skills is the one Trait that will become you and your Co-partners best asset for dealing with all the craziness that's going to come from here on out. You will have issues to discuss between yourselves, your families, possibly between your cultures, religions, and political lives. You will have many decisions to make, without clear choices.

How you deal with this as a couple Having Communication Skills will be crucial test of how you will get along in the marriage. If things aren't going well along these lines, then there are many "couples counseling" and communications courses you should consider. Communication is a skill that can be taught and learned.

It would be better to learn these skills before, as opposed to after getting married.

Fiancé/Fiancée Traits • Having Problem-Solving Skills

Having Problem-Solving Skills will also come to the foreground as you are making marriage, honeymoon, children, living, career and a multitude of other choices that will be coming at you fast and furiously in the upcoming months. Learning to problem-solve in a Win/Win mode is an important tool to enable your relationship to grow and prosper.

❽ NEEDS

Ultimately, the overall need of the courting Co-partner is to find a mate for marriage. It's for the fulfillment of this need that the Boyfriend/Girlfriend Relationships exists. The goal is to find the best possible person with whom to create and share a life as well as build a future family.

It's by going through these last steps of the Boyfriend/Girlfriend Relationship that each Co-partner performs the final testing phase of their best possible choice of a life Co-partner.

Fiancé/Fiancée Needs • Physical

Physically, each Co-partner has a need for:

- A long-term opposite sex relationship
- To be with a healthy Co-partner
- To have (or not have) children
- To share/learn homemaking skills

Fiancé/Fiancée Needs • Emotional

Emotionally, each Co-partner has a need for a Co-partner to:

- Have a relationship he/she can trust will always be there
- Support him/her emotionally
- Be a comfortable combination emotionally

Fiancé/Fiancée Needs • Mental

Mentally, each Co-partner wants a fiancé(e) who:

- Wants to get married
- Has interpersonal skills and understanding
- Shows maturity
- Has a similar moral/spiritual understanding
- Shows potential income earning ability
- Wants to be his/her partner for life

Fiancé/Fiancée Needs • Social

Socially, each Co-partner has a need to:

- Certify his/her status in society's eyes
- Be a good spouse and parent
- Achieve earning power
- Be a social asset in areas such as social prestige
- Be respected in his/her social circles
- Attain and rise in social status
- Express social power and influence
- Share similar religious beliefs

❾ TACTICS

Fiancé/Fiancée Tactics • Positive

Some typically Positive Tactics are:

- Going to pre-marriage counseling course
- Opening discussing all aspects of future together
- Exploring the future through activities with prospective in-laws

Fiancé/Fiancée Tactics • Negative

Some typically Negative Tactics to watch out for are:

- Becoming distant and/or non communicative
- Being hostile or combative around in-laws
- Coping with emotional conflicts through drugs/alcohol
- Letting little problems go until they become big problems
- Not taking care of your side of the seesaw
- Resisting cultural/religious/political steps to marriage

CHAPTER 14

The Husband/Wife Relationship

The Husband/Wife Relationship (marriage) is common to all human societies. When a marriage is stable, it has an extremely positive influence on the health and well-being of the Co-partners; when unstable, the impact is correspondingly negative. The Husband/Wife Relationship (Marriage) is the most complex human relationship. Here's why:

– The Husband/Wife Relationship begins as the logical result of a Boyfriend/Girlfriend Relationship but the dynamics change significantly.

– The Co-partners must learn to live together under the most intimate and complex of circumstances, even though they are not family.

– The union of the two Co-partners merges two different families which creates the resultant responsibilities of an entirely new (and strange) set of In-law/In-law Relationships.

– When the Co-partners produce children, each takes on the equally complex and difficult role as a parent in the new Parent/Child Relationship. This puts pressure on and takes energy away from the existing Husband/Wife Relationship.

– The success of a Parent/Child Relationships is based on a positive interaction within the Husband/Wife Relationship. Children first learn how to be a future spouse by observing and mimicking their parents in action. They suffer as individuals when the relationship between their Father and Mother is strained or filled with tension.

- The Family is the basic unit of society. Marriage is the building block of human societal values with a multi-generational impact on human society. Current marriage relationships are the major influence on the nest generation of children as well as impacting future Parent/Child Relationships down the line.
- The Husband/Wife Relationship goes through several distinct stages, each with varying dynamics.
- The Husband/Wife Relationship has the deepest potential for intimacy (and thus happiness). Although the Co-partners begin the farthest apart (complete strangers/opposite sex), this relationship structure has the most potential for deep intimacy and shared experiences.
- Being happily married may be the single aspect of life most related to personal happiness.

For these reasons and more, the Husband/Wife Relationship is the generic relationship played for the highest stakes with the most to gain and the most to lose.

Husband/Wife Environment

Each couple lives in the Environment of their relationship through their conscious or unconscious decisions. Many factors of the environment specifically impact the marriage relationship.

❶ LOCATION

The Location of the Husband/Wife Relationship is where the couple lives. This includes both their living space along with their immediate neighborhood. Some factors that involve the Location are:

Shelter

- Whether they own or rent an apartment or house
- The decor of their living space
- Their physical possessions such as house wares and furniture
- The amount of living space allotted jointly and individually to each Co-partner

Neighborhood

- The neighborhood where they live
- Transportation factors such as their car(s) or the lack thereof

Other Factors

- Their financial circumstances
- Whether spouses work or don't work
- The circumstances of their job(s)
- Their religious and ethnic background
- The country they live in

Married couples could also have unique variations associated with the location of their relationship. For example, they may:

- Live apart for periods of time
- Live in a motor home or commune
- Have multiple homes
- Be bicoastal
- Be bi-continental

❷ DURATION

Ideally, the Duration of the Husband/Wife Relationship would be for life. Statistically however, this is rare. Perhaps the best predictor of a long-lasting and fulfilling marriage would be the care and the maturity that each Co-partner exhibits during their courtship (Boyfriend/Girlfriend Relationship), combined with the success of each Co-partners respective parent's marriage.

❸ TIMING

The Timing of the Husband/Wife Relationship can be anything from zero up to 24 hours a day. Timing in the marriage relationship is computed when the Co-partners are interacting with each other as Husband/Wife. For example, if a husband and wife work together, the time they spend interacting at work is assigned to their work relationship. The main predictors of the time couples have to spend together are the occupations and social activities of the Co-partners.

Husband/Wife Structure

The Roles in the Husband/Wife Relationship are naturally the Husband and the Wife. Each role has specific duties to perform. In particular, many people want to personalize or contemporize these roles description from what HRW describes. Try to avoid this if you want to understand HRW.

Think of this in the following manner. If both Husband and Wife "can do" the other's job, what are the activities that men can't do or aren't partial to, that woman do well, and vice versa. These differences are what each role description adds to the marriage. Also, these role descriptions are based on the vast majority of marriage interactions in all human societies, not just contemporary social opinion from one modern culture.

❹ ROLES

The generic Role of the Husband is to support his wife physically, emotionally, mentally, and socially within both their marriage and the society in which they choose to live. Because these roles are so complex, some more differentiations are made as to living conditions, contact with the spouse, and support.

Husband Role

Husband Role • Physical

The Physical Pole of the Husband is to:

Home/Living Conditions

Provide or establish domicile which includes:

- Shelter from the environment
- Protection from cold, heat, and predators
- Life energy to pay the bills for basic goods & services, (and/or luxuries?)

Home/External Maintenance

- Be responsible for physical chores and maintaining the home exterior and yard
- Taking out the garbage
- Mowing the lawn
- Taking responsibility for repair of cars and major equipment
- Home maintenance such as painting
- Sharing the housework

Physical Contact with Wife

Engage the wife in:

- Nonsexual physical contact such, as holding, massage, and comforting
- Sexual contact such as intimate caressing and intercourse

Husband Role • Emotional

The Emotional Role of the Husband is to:

Emotional/Living Conditions

Be a husband who can:

- Pay attention and respond appropriately to his wife
- Recognize, respect, and adore his wife
- Recognize and respond to wife's need for emotional security and safety
- Be aware of the his wife's "Father Role" expectations

Emotional Contact with the wife

Give his wife emotional priority in his life:

- Be there to listen
- Offer advice if asked
- Nurture, care for, and romance his wife
- Allow her to have her emotional space

Emotional Support for His Wife

Support his wife emotionally

- Encourage his wife to have a life on her side of the seesaw
- Bring out the good and accept the bad in his wife
- Praise his wife's positive behavior
- Support his wife's dreams and goals

Husband Role • Mental

The Mental Pole of the Husband is to:

Mental/Living Conditions

Be a husband who can:

- Communicate his thoughts and feelings about their Husband/Wife Relationship
- Provide intellectual stimulation
- Strive for Win/Win problem solving
- Provide, his intellectual strength
- Is fair and just
- Gives his wife respect as separate but equal

Mental Contact with the Wife

Interact intellectually, such as:

- Discuss difficult subject areas such as death and politics
- Allow wife the right to her own opinions
- Invite his wife to discuss and share major decision-making

Mental Support for His Wife

Encourage his wife to:

- Explore new areas of meaning to her
- Help and advise her to meet her intellectual needs
- Serve as a sounding board for her intellectual ideas

Husband Role • Social

The Social Role of the Husband is to:

Social/Living Conditions

Be a Husband who will perform his role according to social expectations:

- Attend family and social functions when his presence is indicated or requested by his wife, such as weddings and family get-togethers
- Attend church and funeral functions
- Uphold the social responsibilities related to his marriage and family

Social Contact with the Wife

Enjoy social activities with Wife

- Do things socially they both enjoy
- Treat his wife with respect in public

Social Support for His Wife

- Provide social stability as the family figurehead
- Work to increase family's social standing
- Accept the Wife's family
- Support his Wife's personal social needs

Wife Role

The generic Role of the Wife is support her husband physically, emotionally, mentally, and socially within both the marriage and society. Please note: The wife role typically hears the greater responsibility for child care, cooking, and cleaning.

Wife Role • Physical

The Physical Role of the Wife is to:

Home/Living Conditions

Take care of and manage the home, which includes:

- Taking care of her husband and children
- Home/Internal Maintenance

Be responsible for chores to make the inside of the home as comfortable and inviting as possible, such as:

- Cleaning the house
- Gathering food and preparing meals
- Picking up clothes and doing the wash
- Ironing

Physical contact with the Husband

Engage the husband in:

- Nonsexual physical contact such as holding, massage, and comforting
- Sexual contact such as intimate caressing and intercourse

Wife Role • Emotional

The Emotional Role of the wife is to:

Emotional/Living Conditions

Be a Wife who can:

- Create a harmonious home atmosphere
- Pay attention and respond appropriately to her husband
- Recognize, respect, and adore her husband
- Recognize and respond to her husband's need for emotional security and safety
- Be aware of her husband's "Mother" expectations

Emotional Contact with the Husband

Give her husband emotional priority in her life:

- Be there to listen
- Offer advice if asked
- Nurture, care for, and romance her husband
- Allow him to have his emotional space
- Be a friend and confident for her husband
- Cheer up her husband when he is sad or down

Emotional Support for Her Husband

Support her husband emotionally:

- Encourage her husband to have a life on his side of the see-saw
- Bring out the good and accept the bad in her husband
- Praise her husband's positive behavior
- Support her husband's dreams and goals
- Demonstrate loyalty and support
- Trust and encourage her husband

Wife Role • Mental

The Mental Role of the Wife is to:

Mental/Living Conditions

Be a wife who can:

- Communicate her thoughts and feelings
- Provide intellectual stimulation
- Strive for Win/Win problem-solving
- Provide her intellectual strength
- Respect her husband as separate but equal

Mental Contact with the Wife

Interact intellectually, such as:

- Discuss difficult subject areas such as death and politics
- Allow husband the right to his own opinions
- Discuss and share major decision-making

Mental Support for Her Husband

Encourage her husband to:

- Explore new areas of meaning to him
- Help and advise him to meet his intellectual needs
- Be a sounding board for his intellectual discussions
- Communicate by sharing thoughts and feelings with her husband
- Share his conversation and interests
- Take time to talk things out
- Share and acknowledge the intellectual pursuits of husband as much as practical
- Share and develop her own intellectual concerns and needs with her husband
- Teach her husband
- Stimulate her husband intellectually
- Offer her husband advice when asked or appropriate

Wife Role • Social

The Social Role of the Wife is to:

Social/Living Conditions

Be a Wife who performs her role according to social expectations:

- Support her Husband in their marriage as it relates to society
- Assume major responsibility to bear and care for children
- Be responsible for children and their social obligations

Social Contact with the Husband

Enjoy social activities with Husband:

- Do things socially they both enjoy
- Treat her Husband with respect in public

Social Support for Her Husband

- Accompanies her Husband to important functions involving his work
- Work to increase family's social standing
- Be the social hostess when entertaining at home
- Be accepting of Husband's family
- Support her Husband's individual social needs
- Provides for guests and prepare home for company
- Work to enhance his standing in the community
- Accepts his same sex friends, even if she doesn't like them
- Be a companion for her Husband
- Strive to help her Husband socially
- Works to understand and meet Husband's needs

❺ RULES

Husband Rules

Husband Rules • Physical

The Husband's Physical Rules are:

Home/Living conditions

- Provide life energy to maintain a safe and suitable home or apartment
- Answer the door at night
- Open car door for Wife before self
- Provide life energy to pay bills for goods & services (and/or luxuries)

Home/External Maintenance

- Hold responsibility for household repair and maintenance such as painting
- Help with household chores
- Take out the garbage
- Mow the lawn
- Take responsibility for repair of cars and major equipment

Physical Contact with the Wife

- Touch his Wife intentionally such as holding, massage, and comforting
- Engage his Wife in sexual activity such intimate caressing and intercourse
- Be faithful to his Wife sexually
- Respect his Wife's physical privacy

Husband Rules • Emotional

The Husband's Emotional Rules are:

At Home/Emotional Conditions

- Demonstrate emotional support for his Wife
- Keep confidences
- Disclose personal feelings and problems to his Wife
- Give birthday cards and presents to each other
- Repay debts, favors, and compliments
- Seek ways to reduce any tensions in their marriage
- Negotiate areas of personal space

Emotional Contact with the Wife

Communicate distress or anxiety

- Refrain from the "silent treatment"
- Respect each other's emotional privacy
- Show interest in his V Wife's daily activities
- Address his Wife by her first name
- Remember their wedding anniversary
- Maintain eye contact during conversations

Husband Rules • Mental

The Husband's Mental Rules are:

At Home/Mental Conditions

- Inform his Wife about his personal schedule
- Ask for personal advice
- Discuss financial matters openly with her
- Discuss deeper issues such as sex, death, and politics

Mental Contact with the Wife

- Listen to his Wife carefully
- Ask his Wife for help when he needs it
- Share mental ideas with his wife
- Ask questions, rather than assume he already knows

- Ask Wife if she wants to be included in his plans
- Not seek short term escapes to avoid problems in the relationship

Husband Rules • Social

The Husband's Social Rules are:

- Attend celebrations and social events, involving immediate family
- Attend celebrations and social events, involving in-laws family
- Spend time together, away from home and the children
- Go out to dinner
- Offer to pay for his Wife when going out
- Don't remain silent if your Wife's needs are not being met

When Out Socially with Wife

- Don't stare at or ogle other women in front of his wife
- Don't criticize or air his Wife's dirty laundry in public
- Show affection for his Wife publicly
- Be tolerant of Wife's friends even if he doesn't like them
- Stand up for his Wife in her absence

Wife Rules

Wife Rules • Physical

The Wife's Physical Rules are:

Home/Living Conditions

- Provide life energy to maintain the interior of home, apartment, or living environment

Home/Internal Maintenance

- Cook
- Shop
- Clean
- Take care of the kids

Physical Contact with the Husband

- Stay faithful to her Husband sexually
- Touch her Husband intentionally such holding, massage, and comforting
- Engage her Husband in sexual activity such as intimate caressing and intercourse
- Respect her Husband's physical privacy

Wife Rules • Emotional

The Wife's Emotional Rules are:

At Home/Emotional Conditions

- Demonstrate emotional support for Husband
- Keep confidences
- Disclose personal feelings and problems to Husband
- Give birthday cards and presents to Husband
- Seek ways to reduce any tensions in your marriage
- Negotiate areas of personal space

Emotional Contact with Husband

- Communicate distress or anxiety
- Refrain from the "silent treatment"
- Respect your Husband's emotional privacy
- Show interest in Husband's daily activities
- Address Husband by his first name

- Remember your wedding anniversary
- Maintain eye contact during conversations

Additional Rules for Wife

- Explain your thoughts and feelings
- Stand up for your personal rights
- Don't nag
- Don't feel rejected or undesirable
- Don't fear intimacy

Wife Rules • Mental

The Wife's Mental Rules are:

At Home/Mental Conditions

- Inform her Husband about her personal schedule
- Ask for personal advice
- Discuss financial matters openly with each other
- Discuss sex, death, religion, and politics
- Share news of success with each other

Mental contact with the Husband

- Listen carefully to her Husband
- Ask her Husband for help when she needs it
- Share mental ideas with her Husband
- Ask questions, rather than assume
- Ask her Husband if he wants to be included
- Not seek short term escape to avoid problems in the relationship

Additional Rules for Wife

- Don't let your mind turn into mush due to home and children
- Look for hobbies of personal interest
- Create plans for when kids are grown
- Don't sacrifice meeting your personal needs

Wife Rules • Social

The Wife's Social Rules are:

- Attend celebrations and social events, involving immediate family
- Attend celebrations and social events, involving in-laws family
- Spend time together, away from home and the children
- Go out to dinner
- Don't remain silent if your needs are not being met

When Out Socially with Husband

- Don't flirt or vamp with other men in front of Husband
- Don't criticize or air her Husband's dirty laundry in public
- Show affection for her Husband publicly
- Be tolerant of her Husband's friends
- Stand up for your Husband in his absence

❻ CUSTOMS

The Customs of the Husband/Wife Relationship depend on cultural, political, and religious factors specific to the Co-partners.

Husband/Wife Customs • Cultural

List any aspects of your Husband/Wife Relationship that might be a factor regarding your personal ethnic, social, or racial customs. For example:

- Did you grow up in a land foreign from that of your Co-partner?
- Do you differ in racial or ethnic background?
- Do your role expectations contrast due to parental role models?
- Do any factors of your upbringing contribute to your marriage expectations, such as being brought up in a small town, the East Coast, or a commune?

Husband/Wife Customs • Religious

Are strong religious practices or beliefs an important factor in your Husband/Wife Relationship? For example:

- Are you both from the same religion?
- Do you practice your religion equally?
- Does your religion have customs associated with marriage roles that differ from society's norms?

Husband/Wife Customs • Political

Are strong political beliefs a factor in your Husband/Wife Relationship? For example:

- Are you a radical _____ and your spouse is the opposite?
- Do you and your spouse have any strong disagreements over political ideas?
- Do you share any strong political agendas with your spouse?

Husband/Wife Co-partners

❼ TRAITS

Positive marriages are only possible between Co-partners with positive Traits. Regardless of cultural, political, or religious considerations it is the Traits of the marriage Co-partners that carry the relationship through difficult times. Each trait in the HRW system requires its fullest expression in the Husband/Wife Relationship.

Spouse Traits

Spouse Traits • Being Attracted

Are you attracted to your spouse? Not just physically, but emotionally, mentally, and socially as well? Being Attracted to your Spouse is a process that begins during the courting of the Boyfriend/Girlfriend Relationship. It is very important for this attraction to have strong physical, emotional, and mental components. Without a strong attraction, the Co-partners will be unwilling to stay with each other through the trials, tribulations, and responsibilities of a long-term relationship such as marriage.

Simply liking your marriage Co-partner is possibly the single most important consideration of a lasting marriage. Another condition of the lasting marriage is that your spouse becomes more interesting as your marriage continues. These conditions rely almost entirely upon the emotional and mental qualities of your Co-partner.Whatever level of physical (sexual) attraction began the relationship; this will soon become less important as time passes.

Spouse Traits • Being Committed

Are you committed to your wife as a person as well as your marriage as a structure? Being Committed to your spouse is of primary consideration. Even if the Trait of Being Attracted turns off and on, the Trait of Being Committed will sustain the relationship through hard times. Commitment is also a factor that strongly involves the family, religious, and cultural conditions which play a part in marriage. Being Committed as a spouse is a test of your values and stated purpose in life.

Spouse Traits • Being Genuine

Are you genuine with your wife? Being Genuine with your spouse is imperative in the Husband/Wife Relationship. Keeping secrets or denying your true thoughts and feelings will create barriers, put up walls, and block your communication with each other. You have no hope of keeping an important secret or desire from your spouse. Perhaps he or she might not be aware on the conscious level, but emotionally and mentally a spouse is far more attuned to your state of mind than you realize. Keeping secrets, problems, or other types of important information from your spouse will damage the relationship in a major way. It is better to communicate whatever dark secret, than to live in denial or a lie.

Spouse Traits • Being Trustworthy

Are you completely trustworthy for your spouse? Without trust, a marriage can never be based on a secure foundation. Lack of trust will cause all other interactions of the relationship to be unstable. If you are not trustworthy for your spouse, then you are not trustworthy within your self. You have no greater measure of self-worthiness than your trustworthiness as a spouse.

Spouse Traits • Being Emotionally Mature

Are you emotionally mature in your marriage? When the spouse is mature, a marriage has a much better chance of survival. Being emotionally mature is the most complete way to keep tensions from escalating and destroying the foundation of communication and problem-solving that make a marriage work.

It is important to keep any outbreaks of immaturity from impacting your marriage and destroying your credibility as a human being. Part of being newly-married is that both the Co-partners are, by definition, emotionally immature in their relationship. Only by being married for years does the marriage structure itself develop maturity.

Spouse Traits • Having Communication Skills

Do you practice positive Communication Skills? Do you know how to listen better than anyone else you know? Practicing positive communication skills with your spouse is crucial for the survival of your marriage. Being able to communicate your thoughts, feelings, and needs to your wife is critical for day-to-day interaction and long-term happiness.

Within the confines of the marriage relationship, tiny conflicts can build into major catastrophes. If you are not able to recognize your own levels of irritation and communicate them calmly to your Co-partner, you will permit minor scrapes to escalate into major dramas without even realizing it.

Spouse Traits • Having Problem-Solving Skills

Do you have consummate Problem Solving Skills? You are going to need them in a marriage because you are going to have two kinds of problems on a constant basis. They are:

- Problems between you and your spouse
- Problems you and/or your spouse will have with outside situations

Your skill at problem-solving will be required daily as a spouse. Not only to help you and your spouse to get along, but also to help reduce and solve the problems you will have together with others.

❽ NEEDS

Both Husband and Wife Co-partners have needs that fit into physical, emotional, mental, and social categories. The needs each Co-partner has are the engine that drives the relationship structure. Needs are very closely aligned with the roles for both Co-partners. It is critical to understand that both Co-partners must be aware of and communicate his/her needs in a clear, third-party verifiable manner.

Spouse Needs

Spouse Needs • Physical

Physically, a spouse needs a husband/wife who will:

- Care for him/her
- Care and manage the home
- Clean the house
- Gather and prepare food
- Cook
- Do the laundry
- Iron the clothes
- Comfort and support him/her non-sexually
- Be a sexual lover
- Bear and care for their children
- Protect and nurture their children

Physically, the Wife needs a Husband who will:

- Care for her
- Earn money to provide for basic goods and services (and luxuries)
- Pay the bills
- Provide a domicile and shelter from the environment
- Take good care of her homes exterior
- Take out the garbage
- Mow the lawn regularly
- Clean up around the yard
- Engage in nonsexual physical contact such as holding, massage, and comforting
- Engage in sexual contact such as intimate caressing and intercourse
- Be a responsible father for her children
- Care for the children
- Protect and nurture his children

Spouse Needs • Emotional

Emotionally, the Husband needs a Wife who will:

- Create a harmonious home atmosphere
- Be a friend and confidant
- Demonstrate loyalty and support
- Be there to listen
- Be there to cheer him up when he is down
- Give unconditional trust

Emotionally, the Wife needs a Husband who will:

- Pay attention and respond appropriately to her as a person
- Recognize, respect, and adore her
- Make her feel young, desirable, and alive
- Compliment her
- Respond to her need for emotional security and safety
- Give her emotional priority in his life
- Be there to listen
- Offer advice if asked
- Nurture, care, and romance her
- Allow her emotional space
- Encourage her to have a life of her own
- Bring out the good and accept the bad in her
- Praise her positive behavior
- Support her dreams and goals in life
- Meet or match her positive "Father Role" expectations

Spouse Needs • Mental

Mentally, the Husband needs a Wife who will:

- Communicate her thoughts, feelings, and with him
- Share conversation and interests
- Sit down and talk things out with him
- Share or acknowledge his intellectual pursuits

- Teach him skills and subjects he needs to know
- Stimulate him intellectually
- advise him in his best interests

Mentally, the Wife needs a Husband who will:

- Communicate his thoughts, feelings, and needs to her
- Share conversation and interests
- Provide intellectual stimulation
- Sit down and talk things out with her
- Strive for Win/Win problem-solving
- Be responsible for making major decisions
- Be fair and just
- Respect her as separate, but equal
- Share or acknowledge her intellectual pursuits
- Teach her skills and subjects she knows
- Stimulate her intellectually
- Advise her in her best interests

Spouse Needs • Social

Socially, the Husband needs a Wife who will:

- Support him in marriage as it relates to society
- Accompany him to important functions involving his work
- Prepare the house for the arrival of company
- Increase his standing in the community
- Provide for his children and social obligations
- Accept his same sex friends
- Be a companion for him
- Be someone on whom he can depend
- Understand and meet his needs
- Enhance his income earning potential
- Share a lifestyle he is happy with
- Support his social traditions
- Provide for guests

Socially, the Wife needs a Husband who will:

- Be responsible for his role in social interactions with society
- Provide social stability as a figurehead
- Play the Husband role according to the social customs of her family group
- Attend family and social functions, such as weddings and family holidays
- Attend church and funeral functions
- Increase the family's social standing
- Be accepting of her family
- Uphold personal responsibilities to himself as well as those related to his marriage and family.
- Treat her respectfully in public
- Provide for her children and social obligations
- Accept her same sex friends
- Be a companion for her
- Be someone on whom she can depend
- Understand and meet her social needs
- Enhance her income earning potential
- Share a lifestyle she is happy with
- Support her social traditions
- Be civil in front of guests

❾ TACTICS

It is critically important to understand the behavior of both Co-partners as the Tactics they are using to meet their personal needs. Often, the recipient of a negative behavior (tactic) takes it as a personal attack which forces him/her to come up with an opposing tactic to defeat the attack. The negative behavior of a Co-partner is not usually evaluated for what it is; a method the other spouse is using to meet his/her personal needs.

The behavior of the Co-partner (his/her tactics) must be evaluated objectively to determine how a problem can be resolved (a need can be met). How do you tell if a Co-partner's tactics are negative or positive? The answer is third-party verifiable standards. If a Co-partner's Tactics are deemed positive by third-party verifiable standards, this means that person is being positive.

By objectifying the words and actions of your spouse in this way, the deeper issues of working together to build equity in the marriage can he established. Both Husband and Wife want their needs met. To accomplish this goal, each Co-partner must, by necessity, choose some sort of tactic to meet his/her need.

When a Co-partner uses positive Tactics to meet his/her needs, the relationship will be more positive and fulfilling. If the Co-partner uses negative tactics, the relationship will be damaged even if the Co-partner winds up getting his/her needs met!

Spouse Tactics

Spouse Tactics • Positive

Positive Tactics used by both Co-partners, is a fundamental requirement for the success of a Husband/Wife Relationship. Honest and direct communication from the Co-partner is the key to using positive tactics. This requires two things:

- The spouse knows what it is he or she wants (the PEMS need)
- The spouse knows how to communicate his/her need in a positive manner.

Positive Tactics can be developed in many ways if the person has positive Traits in order to want to use positive Tactics in the first place. Positive Tactics may be learned by studying communication methods and relationship dynamics.

Whether the positive Tactics come from each other, a television show, a therapist, a self-help hook, or a magazine article doesn't really matter. What does matter is that each Co-partner uses the most conscious and positive Tactics possible to meet his/her needs.

Some examples of positive tactics that the Spouse can use:

- Surprise your spouse with a "no occasion" gift
- Call once in a while during the day to see how your spouse is doing
- Initiate an occasional non-sexual cuddle or hug session
- Make an effort to correct habits or behaviors that displease your spouse
- Forgive your spouse when he/she has been hurtful
- Pay attention and respond appropriately to your spouse's communication and moods
- Share an interest of your spouse with your spouse
- Volunteer to take over some of the chores when spouse is not feeling well
- Communicate your needs in a third-party verifiable manner
- Suggest solutions and optional behaviors rather than just blaming or using put-downs

Spouse Tactics • Negative

The constant use of negative tactics will eventually destroy any relationship. If a Co-partner's Tactics are deemed negative by third-party verifiable standards, this certifies that the person is being negative. Most conflicts in the Husband/Wife Relationship are created when one Co-partner uses Tactics deemed negative by the other.

Some obvious examples are:

- Keeping important facts or information from your spouse
- Physically hitting or striking your spouse
- Verbally abusing your spouse with negative put downs
- Blaming or putting down a spouse to build own ego
- Dwelling on problems, not solutions

Sometimes, the Tactics used by a Co-partner are so obviously ineffective or hostile that they can only point to a deeper personal problem of the spouse.

CHAPTER 15

The In-law/In-law Relationships

In-laws intersect the two most primal and intimate relationships: the Parent/Child and the Husband/Wife Relationships. In-law/In-law Relationship can be a source of stress for either or both sets of Co-partners. The roles experiencing the most difficulty are often the Husband with his Mother-In-Law since the dynamics of the marital bond are in direct conflict with the strongest Parent/Child bond (mother and daughter).

In-law/In-law Relationships are a reminder that, in marriage, you are marrying your spouse's entire family, not just your spouse. You may be forced to interact and be nice to people with whom you have or share no history. As well, there will be an extensive family history that already precedes you about which you know nothing.

Since you don't decide on your In-laws, this relationship may be one of the most difficult relationships in which to have a mutually-satisfying experience. The In-laws also present the possibility of many potential troubles sources since there could be an additional two parents, possible siblings, and maybe even kin members of the In-law family who will want to add their opinions to the mix.

In-law/In-law Environment

❶ LOCATION

The Location of the In-law/In-law Relationship is wherever the interactions take place. If the In-laws live more than 100 miles away, chances are you won't see them that often. If, however, they live in the next room you will see them several times a day.

Often, it is convenient for the newly-weds to live with their In-laws. The parents will have a built-in support system for the couple to settle in which makes it easier for them to begin saving money for their own home and furnishings. In many cultures this arrangement is common, even expected.

❷ DURATION

The Duration of the In-law/In-law Relationship continues as long as the couple is married. It's possible that if you do get divorced, depending on the Co-partners involved, you may remain in contact with Ex-In-laws, but it's not the norm.

❸ TIMING

The Timing of the In-law/In-law Relationship will depend on the proximity of the In-laws. Typically, the married couple might see the In-laws for dinner or a barbecue once a week or twice a month. They might see each other more frequently if children are involved. Often, the In-laws are willing to provide baby-sitting and other support services for the married couple. If the In-laws live far away they might only see each other sporadically or at special events such as holidays and the birth of children.

In-law/In-law Structure

❹ ROLES

The In-law/In-law Relationships include many different roles. The individual Roles of the In-law/In-are:

- Mother-in-law
- Father-in-law
- Daughter-in-law
- Son-in-law
- Sister-in-law
- Brother-in-law

This can create quite a number of primary in-law relationships depending on the specifics of the family involved:

- Mother-in-law/Daughter-in-law
- Mother-in-law/Son-in-law
- Father-in-law/Daughter-in-law
- Father-in-law/Son-in-law
- Sister-in-law/Sister-in-law
- Brother-in-law/Brother-in-law
- Sister-in-law/Brother-in-law

Parents-in-law Role

Ideally, the Role of the Parents-in-law is to make life easier for the newlyweds. These Roles typically involve ways in which the In-laws can support each other.

Parents-in-law Role • Physical

The role of the Parents-in-law could involve:

- Baby sitting the children
- Supporting the son/daughter-in-law in practical ways, such as doing laundry or helping around the house

---

- Supporting the son/daughter-in-law financially via money, equipment, or supplies
- Be there for emergencies

Parents-in-law Role • Emotional

- Support the son/daughter-in-law emotionally
- Make him/her feel welcome into the family
- Greet him/her with acceptance
- Don't interfere in the affairs of the son/daughter-in-law
- Don't involve the son/daughter-in-laws in their own emotional problems

Parents-in-law Role • Mental

- Don't take sides in family disputes
- Educate and help the son/daughter-in-law with knowledge and information
- Advise them where and how to get supplies and bargains
- Communicate with the couple
- Be mindful of the potential the relationship has to offer
- Don't judge negatively

Parents-in-law Role • Social

- Introduce the son/daughter-in-law to the family circle
- Invite the son/daughter-in-law to family gatherings
- Speak to and about the son/daughter-in-law in a positive manner
- Include the son/daughter-in-law into their plans
- Support the son/daughter-in-law when they are not there
- Try to make initial years of marriage positive
- Don't smother the new son/daughter-in-law
- Don't be hypocritical or backstabbing
- Be understanding that you are gaining not losing a family member
- Create quality time when together

- Accept the new In-law as a family member even if he/she is someone you don't like or approve

Son/Daughter-in-law Role

Son/Daughter-in-law Role • Physical

- Use skills to help In-laws
- Utilize the skills of family members

Son/Daughter-in-law Role • Emotional

- Don't judge or compare your In-laws to your parents
- Don't try to prevent access of your wife/husband to his/her parents
- Don't bear grudges against In-laws
- Don't let In-law pressures strain the marriage
- Don't create resentment or conflicts since In-laws never forget

Son/Daughter-in-law Role • Mental

- Be respectful of your elders
- Remember that your In-laws are different
- Don't be afraid to defend your boundaries but be able to compromise
- Beware of conflicts between the two sets of In-laws
- Be courteous and respectful even if you don't always agree with your In-laws

Son/Daughter-in-law Role • Social

- Don't try to change your In-laws since they have a history and were probably brought up differently
- Practice your communication skills of listening and communicating your thoughts, feelings, and needs
- Be aware that if living with your Parents-in-law, you are living under their rules and by their system
- Be considerate of your In-laws privacy

Sibling-in Law Role

Sibling-in Law Role • Physical

Sibling-in Law Role • Emotional

Sibling-in Law Role • Mental

Sibling-in Law Role • Social

❺ RULES

Parents-In-law Rules

Parents-In-law Rules • Physical

Physically, the Parents-In-Law should:

- Offer help with moving or other manual chores
- Not engage in sexual activity

Parents-In-law Rules • Emotional

Emotionally, the Parents-In-Law should:

- Show him/her emotional support
- Share news of success with him/her
- Remember his/her birthday
- Keep his/her confidences
- Maintain eye contact with him/her
- Address him/her by his/her first name
- Avoid proximity in living arrangements

Parents-In-law Rules • Mental

Mentally, the Parents-In-Law should:

- Help him/her with advice or knowledge
- Be willing to introduce him/her to personal contacts
- Offer help and advice if asked
- Respect the bond between your son/daughter and his/her spouse
- Don't interfere in the new couple's domestic issues

Parents-In-law Rules • Social

Socially, the Parents-In-Law should:

- Respect the new couple's privacy
- Invite the new couple to family celebrations
- Work to establish good relations with the other In-laws
- Don't criticize either him/her in public
- Stand up for the new couple in their absence

Son/Daughter-in-law Rules

Son/Daughter-in-law Rules • Physical

Physically, the Daughter/Son-In-law should:

- Offer to help or assist your In-laws with physical chores
- Not engage in sexual activity
- If living with the In-laws, don't make a mess
- If living with In-laws, don't expect them to clean up after you

Son/Daughter-in-law Rules • Emotional

Emotionally, the Daughter/Son-In-law should:

- Strive to make the In-laws feel welcome in your home
- Remember their birthdays, anniversaries, and special occasions
- Bring your parents-in-law the occasional gift

Son/Daughter-in-law Rules • Mental

Mentally, the Daughter/Son-In-law should:

- Respect the position and authority of your In-laws
- Ask for guidance and advice when appropriate
- Keep in mind there is a major history to this family before you ever arrived
- Help your In-laws with your special skills

Son/Daughter-in-law Rules • Social

Socially, the Daughter/Son-In-law should:

- Visit your In-laws regularly
- Support and assist your parents-in-law in their old age
- Invite your In-laws to family celebrations
- Praise your In-laws when appropriate
- Don't take In-laws support for granted
- Don't let In-law interactions turn into ego battles
- Take special care to only worry about your side of the see-saw

❻ CUSTOMS

In-law Customs • Cultural

Here is where some real issues can arise if your spouse's parents are from a different country and social structure. This includes factors such as their age, their economic status, where which is living, country vs. city, and many other permutations of factors that have the potential to become problematic.

In-law Customs • Religious

Religion, especially for the parents-in-law can also be a true mine field. Even if your spouse is not religious, this might be where the parents-in-law see it as their duty to turn things around for the "sake of the children" that might not even be born yet.

There are so many potential areas of conflict that it would be fruitless to begin outlining them all. Just know that if you are suddenly in a major conflict with your In-laws, and your spouse is on their side, that somewhere in this section of customs you are going to have a place to describe the situation you are facing.

In-law Customs • Political

Again, the devil is in the details. Are your parents-in-law politically emotive? Does this involve current politics or the way things used to be? If you are the parent-in-law, is your new son-in-law a prominent Republican, and you've been a Democrat all your life? Or perhaps you are a criminal defense attorney and your new Father-in-law is the Chief of Police.

In-law/In-law Co-partners

Here is where the luck of the draw enters your life. Hopefully you have met the In-laws and you know them quite well. Or perhaps, you are meeting them for the first time on your wedding day.

❼ TRAITS

In-law Traits

In-law Co-partners Traits • Being Attracted

When it happens Being Attracted is an excellent Trait for the In-law/In-law Relationship. At first you were attracted to your spouse. Once you get married the In-laws come with the deal. If you like and are attracted to your In-laws you are lucky. If you dislike your In-laws intensely then your relationship will be much more difficult. Of course, this applies for your In-laws as well. They may or may not be attracted to you.

In-law Co-partners Traits • Being Committed

Being Committed to your In-laws is implied on the basis of being married to your spouse. This means that you are willing to be part of the social system of your new family when appropriate, such as attending family gatherings and holiday celebrations. You will have to learn how juggle your potentially contrasting commitments since your parents will want the same respect and commitment from your spouse as well.

In-law Co-partners Traits • Being Genuine

The In-law/In-law Relationship is one relationship where you want to stress etiquette, formality, and good manners. If your true thoughts, feelings, and needs are positive and fit in with your In-laws, you will be welcome to share them. However, if your relationship is a difficult one, you would be pragmatic to keep your negative thoughts and feelings to yourself while striving to maintain civility such as in the Chinese tradition. There is no way to win a conflict with your In-laws, even when you are right.

In-law Co-partners Traits • Being Trustworthy

Your ability to be trustworthy will be a most important Trait in your In-law/In-law Relationship. You will have many opportunities to test your In-laws on this trait as well. It is particularly important that you not take undue advantage of your In-laws. If they are generous with their support, make sure to let them know you are appreciative of their efforts on your behalf. If you are the parents-In-law, be aware that while you have had many years to accumulate your standard of living, a young couple can not be expected to provide themselves with an equal standard of living.

In-law Co-partners Traits • Being Emotionally Mature

Ideally, the parents-in-law will be positive, emotionally mature adults who are happy and content with their own lives and are looking forward to the benefits that a positive In-law Relationship can provide. Thus, they will be happy with their new son/daughter-in-law and look forward to having grandchildren. By definition, the newlyweds are going to be immature. They will have many difficult adjustments to make just getting used to their new marriage. If the parents-in-law are needy and immature, this will place an additional burden on the new marriage.

In-law Co-partners Traits • Having Communication Skills

Having Communication Skills is especially valuable in the In-law/In-law Relationship. Many problems that develop will begin with unclear or miscommunication between the Co-partners. Each side of the relationship must strive to keep their communication open and clear to reduce the potential levels of stress.

In-law Co-partners Traits • Having Problem-Solving Skills

If problems develop, and they will, problem-solving skills will be needed. Problem-solving is difficult to attain if the parents-in-law are immature and making unreasonable demands on the new couple. Don't think it doesn't happen.

Any In-law problems also have the potential of creating stress between the Co-partners of the Husband/Wife Relationship. Special care must be taken by all parties to resolve problems quickly rather than letting them linger to grow into long-standing feuds. There's already enough of these.

❽ NEEDS

Parents-In-law Needs

Parents-In-law Needs • Physical

Physically, the Parents-In-law need a Son/Daughter-In-law who will:

- Use his/her skills to help them out
- Utilize the skills of family members
- Care for them as they age

Parents-In-law Needs • Emotional

Emotionally, the Parents-In-law need a Son/Daughter-In-law who will:

- Not judge or compare In-laws to own parents
- Not try to prevent access of son/daughter to parents
- Not hold grudges against In-laws
- Not be emotionally immature with In-laws
- Not try to create resentment

Parents-In-law Needs • Mental

Mentally, the Parents-In-law need a Son/Daughter-In-law who will:

- Be respectful
- Not be afraid to defend his/her boundaries without being unreasonable
- Be courteous and respectful

Parents-In-law Needs • Social

Socially, the Parents-In-law need a Son/Daughter-In-law who will:

- Accept that they have a history and were raised differently
- Have positive communication skills
- If living in their house, be aware that he/she is living under their rules and by their system
- Be respectful of their privacy.

Son/Daughter-In-law Needs

Son/Daughter-In-law Needs • Physical

Physically, the Son/Daughter-In-law needs Parents-in-law who will:

- Baby sits the kids
- Support him/her in practical ways such as washing or helping with home maintenance
- Support him/her financially through money, equipment, or supplies
- Be there as a backup for an emergency

Son/Daughter-In-law Needs • Emotional

Emotionally the Son/Daughter-In-law needs Parents-in-law who will:

- Support him/her emotionally
- Make him/her feel welcome into the family
- Greet him/her with acceptance
- Not interfere in his/her affairs
- Not drag him/her into their own emotional problems

Son/Daughter-In-law Needs • Mental

Mentally the Son/Daughter-In-law needs Parents-in-law who will:

- Not take sides in family disputes
- Educate and help him/her with their knowledge
- Show him/her where to purchase supplies or get bargains
- Be mindful of the potential the relationship has to offer
- Not judge him/her negatively

Son/Daughter-In-law Needs • Social

Socially, the Son/Daughter-In-law needs Parents-in-law who will:

- Introduce and welcome him/her into the family circle
- Invite him/her to family gatherings
- Talk about him/her in a positive manner
- Include him/her into their plans
- Make their initial years of marriage a positive experience
- Not smother their new relationship
- Not backstab him/her
- Understand they are gaining not losing a family member
- Create quality time when together
- Not resent him/her even if he/she is someone they don't like or approve

❾ TACTICS

In-law Tactics

Mothers-in-law are more likely to give things while mothers are more likely to do things for married daughters.

In-law Tactics • Positive

Some Positive Tactics of the Parents-In-Law are:

-
-

Some Positive Tactics of the Son/Daughter-In-Law are:

–

–

Some Positive Tactics of the Brother/Sister-In-Law are:

–

–

In-law Tactics • Negative

Some Negative Tactics of the Parents-In-Law are:

–

–

Some Negative Tactics of the Son/Daughter-In-Law are:

–

–

Some Negative Tactics of the Brother/Sister-In-Law are:

–

–

In-law Tactics • Miscellaneous

With the In-law/In-Law Relationship, you must decide a balance of contact between:

–   What you would like
–   What you can tolerate
–   What is practical
–   What is healthy
–   What your In-laws want
–   What your spouse wants
–   How much does your spouse like visiting your parents
–   How close or far away do you in-laws live

CHAPTER 16

The Neighbor/Neighbor Relationship

The Neighbor/Neighbor Relationship establishes the foundation for the relationships that create human society and is also important on a practical level. The people you live next to can have a strong influence on your happiness and peace of mind. Neighbors can become a source of irritation through excessive noise, privacy or pet problems, or other instances of interference. Neighbors are also your first line of assistance if a major emergency arises.

The Neighbor/Neighbor Relationship has the potential to be one of the weakest personal bonds in HRW since its sole basis is a person or family lives next to you. On the other hand, if someone lives next door, you have a better opportunity to know them intimately, if you so desire.

Neighbor/Neighbor Environment

The Environment of the Neighbor/Neighbor Relationships is easy; where you live. It also includes additional layers, such as your street, your neighborhood, your postcode, your suburb, your city, your state, and your country.

❶ LOCATION

The Location of the Neighbor/Neighbor Relationship is the initiating circumstance creating the relationship as well as the main factor enforcing your cooperation. It is defined by the general boundaries of your property line. This may mean a specific grouping of houses, apartments, or condominiums or a more rural area with associated schools and shopping centers.

Your immediate neighbors are either next-door or back-to-back. The next group would be those who live on your street. Additionally neighbors may be met through local school or neighborhood watch meetings, church, sports, or social clubs. If you live in an apartment, or condo, a school dorm, or even have what Australian's call flat mates, then these are your neighbors for the purposes of this discussion.

❷ DURATION

The Duration of the Neighbor/Neighbor Relationship exists for as long as you and your neighbors live in that location although you may not have an active relationship with your neighbors.

❸ TIMING

The Timing involves the amount of time you spend interacting with your neighbors. You may meet frequently in each other's home, merely greet each other once in a while, or never interact at all. If you are living with a roommate then you might be in the same room with them for hours at a time.

Neighbor/Neighbor Structure

The Structure of the Neighbor/Neighbor Relationship is important to keep in mind when differentiating between neighbors and friends. Neighbors can seem quite like friends in many ways, but they may not react to you like a friend. Or, you may have a neighbor who makes the assumption that you are his/her friend, and therefore takes liberties with which you don't feel comfortable.

❹ ROLES

A Neighbor is a person you may see regularly in the course of your neighborhood activities, but who is not close enough to be considered a personal friend. These activities might include:

- Speaking to your neighbor while washing your car
- Seeing them while shopping
- Visiting to borrow a tool or ask for advice
- Discussing security at a neighborhood watch meeting
- Commenting on the weather with the neighborhood shop keepers
- Other forms of casual contact

Neighbors maintain order in their immediate area and take joint action to monitor neighborhood problems or outside threats. Neighbors also exert peer pressure on fellow neighbors to maintain appearances of the house and yard and to "keep up with the Jones" in material possessions. Neighbors share local gossip and chit chat. Neighborhood wives often have coffee parties or entertain neighborhood friends.

Another important neighbor role is providing mutual assistance especially in areas such as baby-sitting, car problems, medical referrals, and gardening. Many neighbors interact through participation in voluntary associations such as athletic or service clubs, parent-teacher associations, church or social clubs, anonymous support groups, or evening classes.

Neighbor Role

Neighbor Role • Physical

Physically, the Role of a Neighbor is to:

- Be willing to help in an emergency
- Be considerate about noise
- Be considerate about pets, such as barking dogs
- Be considerate about children
- Notify neighbors about activities such as parties
- Be watchful of each other's children and houses when others are away
- Maintain property according to neighborhood standards
- Protect neighborhood property
- Not trespass on neighbor's property
- Be helpful if requested by a neighbor to water plants or pick up mail during their absence
- Be willing to loan tools or items if this privilege is not abused
- Return borrowed items such as tools
- Respect each other's property rights
- Not steal from the garden, shed, or trees
- Not enter neighbors home uninvited

Neighbor Role • Emotional

Emotionally the Role of a Neighbor is to:

- Make an effort to become acquainted, such as bringing over cakes
- Not feel free to take as much of the other's time as one desires
- Be willing to exchange a few social words
- Be willing to help with small problems
- Not interfere with each other's personal problems

Neighbor Role • Mental

Mentally, the Role of a Neighbor is to:

- Respect each other's privacy
- Keep confidences
- Not encroach over shared boundaries
- Repay debts or favors
- Share information sources, such as for household repairs

Neighbor Role • Social

Socially, the Role of a Neighbor is to:

- Always greet each another in public
- Attend neighborhood meetings
- Rally to protect or defend neighborhood from outside problems
- Welcome new neighbors to the neighborhood
- Inform the neighbors when you are having a party
- Assist with neighborhood maintenance

❺ RULES

Neighbor Rules

Neighbor Rules • Physical

Physically, the Rules of a Neighbor are to:

- Be willing to help in an emergency
- Be considerate about noise
- Be considerate about pets, such as barking dogs
- Be considerate about children
- Notify neighbors about activities such as parties
- Be watchful of each other's children and houses when others are away

- Maintain your property according to neighborhood standards
- Protect neighborhood property
- Not trespass on neighbor's property
- Be helpful if requested by a neighbor to water plants or pick up mail during their absence
- Be willing to loan tools or items if this privilege is not abused
- Return borrowed items such as tools
- Respect each other's property rights
- Not steal from the garden, shed, or trees
- Not enter neighbors home uninvited

Neighbor Rules • Emotional

Emotionally, the Rules of a Neighbor are to:

- Make an effort to become acquainted, such as bringing over cakes
- Not feel free to take as much of the other's time as one desires
- Be willing to exchange a few social words
- Be willing to help with small problems
- Not interfere with each other's personal problems

Neighbor Rules • Mental

Mentally, the Rules of a Neighbor are to:

- Respect each other's privacy
- Keep confidences
- Not encroach over shared boundaries
- Repay debts or favors
- Share information sources, such as for household repairs

Neighbor Rules • Social

Socially, the Rules of a Neighbor are to:

- Always greet each another in public
- Attend neighborhood meetings
- Rally to protect or defend neighborhood from outside problems
- Welcome new neighbors to the neighborhood
- Inform neighbors when having a party
- Assist with neighborhood maintenance

❻ CUSTOMS

Neighbor Customs • Cultural

-
-

Neighbor Customs • Religious

-
-

Neighbor Customs • Political

-
-

Neighbor/Neighbor Co-partners

❼ TRAITS

Since neighbors are a less intimate relationship, specific traits of your Co-partner can turn this relationship into even more of a fiasco, because your neighbor interactions might revolve around that trait only. For example, you teenage neighbor plays rock music really loud at night. His parents aren't home, so they don't care. Or the leaves from your tree are falling on your neighbor's grass, so he's filing a lawsuit about it.

The Neighbor/Neighbor Relationship can become an unbelievable nightmare for some people because of the confined space. There's not much you can do either because neither of you wants to move.

The ideal neighbor would have the positive HRW Traits and can make your life very pleasant. The way you might notice this is that you don't have trouble with your neighbors, but you have a lot of friends who do. Or you might have the "John Belushi" type neighbor, and no matter what you do, every day there is going to be a new drama to consider.

Neighbor Traits

Neighbor Traits • Being Attracted

Through your close proximity, you will have many opportunities to meet and interact with your close neighbors. If you like each other, you will probably explore your relationship further, perhaps turning it into a Friend/Friend Relationship. If you don't like him/her, then you will probably speak only briefly or not at all.

Neighbor Traits • Being Committed

Being Committed in the Neighbor/Neighbor Relationship is more a matter of being committed to the welfare of your property and the neighborhood in general.

Neighbor Traits • Being Genuine

You may want to monitor this trait when communicating with your neighbors. For example, you may have certain thoughts and feelings, yet if you tell them to your neighbor, he or she might hate you for life. Since you live in close proximity, "keeping the peace" is an overall priority. Yet, being genuine is always preferable to agreeing to do things you don't want to do or living a lie that bothers your conscience.

Neighbor Traits • Being Trustworthy

Being Trustworthy in the Neighbor/Neighbor Relationship means things like not stealing from your neighbors. Another example is agreeing to borrow tools and returning them in good condition as soon as you are finished with them.

Neighbor Traits • Being Emotionally Mature

Being Emotionally Mature is a bonus in the Neighbor/Neighbor Relationship. In this situation neighbors are considerate of each other's needs, such as reducing noise levels at night, not mowing the lawn at 6:00 in the morning, etc.

Neighbor Traits • Having Communication Skills

Specific Communication Skills are often needed when communicating with your neighbor. You might have some very uncomfortable circumstances to discuss. The more practiced you are with communication skills, the more likely your needs will he met.

Neighbor Traits • Having Problem-Solving Skills

Problem-Solving Skills are crucial in the Neighbor/Neighbor Relationship. This relationship has a tendency to bring out the worst in the Co-partners when their problems go unresolved. Many times unresolved problems escalate to lengthy and expensive-court battles or even violence.

❽ NEEDS

Neighbors have needs that characteristically require assistance, especially if they are older or are married with children.

Neighbor Needs

Neighbor Needs • Physical

Physically, a Neighbor needs other Neighbors who will:

- Be willing to control problems with noise, boundaries, and declining property values
- Assist with chores such as babysitting, household maintenance, or yard work
- Be willing to help in an emergency
- Be considerate about noise
- Be considerate about pets, such as barking dogs
- Be considerate about children
- Notify neighbors about activities such as parties
- Be watchful of each other's children and houses when others are away
- Maintain your property according to neighborhood standards
- Protect neighborhood property
- Not trespass on neighbor's property
- Be helpful if requested by a neighbor to water plants or pick up mail during their absence
- Be willing to loan tools or items if this privilege is not abused
- Return borrowed items such as tools
- Respect each other's property rights
- Not steal from the garden, shed, or trees
- Not enter neighbors home uninvited

Neighbor Needs • Emotional

Emotionally, a Neighbor needs other Neighbors who will:

- Serve as a companion for conversation
- Remain friendly but not necessarily close
- Make an effort to become acquainted, such as bringing over cakes or cookies
- Not feel free to take as much of the other's time as one desires
- Be willing to take time to exchange a few social words
- Be willing to help with small problems
- Not interfere with each other's personal problems

Neighbor Needs • Mental

Mentally, a Neighbor needs other Neighbors who will:

- Respect each other's privacy
- Keep confidences
- Not encroach over shared boundaries
- Repay debts or favors
- Share information sources, such as for household repairs

Neighbor Needs • Social

Socially, a Neighbor needs other Neighbors who will:

- Embrace and share the concept of civic commitment
- Always greet each another in public
- Attend neighborhood meetings
- Rally to protect or defend neighborhood from outside problems
- Welcome new neighbors to the neighborhood
- Inform neighbors when having a party
- Assist with neighborhood maintenance

❾ TACTICS

Neighbor Tactics

The positive Tactics of a neighbor would mean that he/she was closely following the rules. Particularly in the Neighbor/Neighbor Relationship following the rules sums up the tactical skills required in the relationship.

Neighbor Tactics • Positive

Some positive tactics for a Neighbor would be

- Asking the other Neighbor if they need assistance in any way
- Keeping the lawn or external environment neat and tidy
- Clearing their garbage bins on the proper days
- Keeping excessive noise to a minimum

Neighbor Tactics • Negative

Some negative tactics for a Neighbor would be

- Never speaking or acknowledging the other neighbor, even in his/her presence
- Having 5 pit bulls chained to the tree in their yard
- Having parties to all hours
- Selling drugs with frequent customers coming and going at all hours
- "Borrowing" your tools or lawn mower and never giving them back

PART TWO: SECTION THREE

INTRO TO
WORK RELATIONSHIPS

CHAPTER 17

*T*he Boss/Employee Relationship

In many ways, the Boss/Employee Relationships is the primary work relationship and is also the one that gives people the most grief. One reason is that this relationship acts as a substitute Parent/Child Relationship for many people. The aspects of power that a Boss holds are in many ways similar to that of a Parent.

Another factor is, as people continue to replace what's real in their life with money, their Boss becomes the superficial source of the major thing they care about. So, if they have trouble with their Boss, this means trouble with their money.

When I first started consulting others on their "relationship problems" I was shocked to learn how much Work relationships were a primary problem on most people's minds.

I'm sure part of the concern is due to the fact that these relationships involve money.

It's also true that for many of us, being a Co-partner as an Employee and/or a Co-worker is where we have the least meaningful influence on our side of the seesaw.

Boss/Employee Environment

The Work Environment may be the dominant factor of the relationship as in working in a coal mine. Or, the Environment may be incidental, such as working in an office. Many people that dislike their job might find that they actually dislike the Environmental element more than any other factor. Perhaps it's the distance they have to drive, or the conditions of their work place, or what they have to breathe when they are at work.

It's important to assess your work place by considering just the Environmental aspects and nothing else.

❶ LOCATION

The Location of the Boss/Employee Relationship is the work place, such as an office, factory, or school. Wherever a person reports to work and actually performs his/her job represents the immediate work location. The Location of your job may place you inside a Wall Street broker's office or chasing gorillas in Rwanda. Your job may be inside a secretarial pool or climbing telephone poles outside in the snow.

Where's the Boss?

One factor of your Work Location is where does your Boss sit and where is this in relation to you? Or if you are the Boss, where do your Employees work? Many possibilities exist for the Boss Location. For example, your Boss may be far from the Location where you perform your work. (You may be a journalist stationed in a foreign country). Or you may be a Boss who works in the same room as your Employees. (You are a real estate agent.) You may work for an oil company and your boss is in Mexico City and yet you work from Villahermosa.

Additional Factors of the Work Environment

A further delineation of the work environment is represented by the conditions under which you work. Such factors that impact the Boss/Employee Environment are:

- Cleanliness of the work place
- Quality of the equipment
- Address location of the building
- The emotional environment surrounding the work place
- The mental (creative and intellectual) Environment surrounding the work place
- The social Environment surrounding the work place
- The reputation of your job, your company, your industry

Other factors of the work Environment Location involve those that you bring to the job such as:

- The clothes you wear (or must wear) for the job
- The length of time it takes you to get to work
- Your transportation costs to and from work
- The type of people who are your Coworkers
- How you react to the particular stresses of this job

❷ DURATION

Duration is the length of time you have been working at that job with the specific Co-partner. One aspect to keep in mind is that you may have been working at one company for ten years but you were an Employee for 6 years and then a Boss for 4 years. This also means, of course, that you have changed relationship structures as well.

Just because you've worked at the same company for ten years doesn't mean that you might not have had several different Boss/Employee relationships, with you as the Co-partner being on both sides of the seesaw in several different Environments.

❸ TIMING

Timing in the Boss/Employee Relationship involves such factors as when you go to work. Are the job hours from 6:00 a.m. to 3:00 pm or do you work the midnight shift? Do you interact with your Boss all day every day, or only 1 times a quarter when it's quarterly report time. Perhaps email is your primary method of communication, or the phone, or telex.

In general it's a good idea to have a conscious understanding of specifically when, how long, and how many times that you and your Boss actually interact during a specific period of time. I worked for a company for a year and half and never once did the Boss discuss my job or what he wanted me to do.

Boss/Employee Structure

Two different Roles create the Boss/Employee Structure: the Boss role and the Employee role. This structure has been explored in detail and is tightly defined by society. Although HRW presents the basic guidelines, many companies have complex manuals defining this relationship down to minute details.

Yet Boss/Employee Relationships also exist where there is no delineation of the roles and rules at all for the Two Co-partners.

❹ ROLES

Boss Role

A major Role of the Boss is leadership and teaching. His authority is to train, advise, and manage Employees to achieve task-oriented business goals. Although both Co-partners have equal weight as far as the relationship seesaw is concerned, the Boss has many responsibilities for the success of the relationship that are on his/her side of the seesaw alone.

Since, the Boss is in a dominant position; the Boss is perceived and treated differently by Employees. Being a boss mandates a prescribed set of behaviors. He/she is responsible to produce a product or service and is accountable for the performance of all Employees under his/her jurisdiction.

For this reason the Boss can never be "one of the gang." This presents a problem when a former worker from the ranks is promoted to the Boss role. In these circumstances a boss may be forced to discipline, reprimand, or even fire former Coworkers. Employees will not make it easy on the Boss because it is not to their advantage.

Boss Role • Physical

Physically, the role of the Boss is to:

- Create a pleasant and productive work environment where Employees can feel good about their work as well as each other
- Fit Employees to the job and establish standards of quality and production
- Be responsible for making sure that Employees get paid
- Protect Employees from physical harm

Boss Role • Emotional

Emotionally, the role of the Boss is to:

- Recognize and reward Employees for work well done
- Support Employees emotionally in regards to work objectives
- Inspire Employees through example
- Be tolerant of Employee mistakes during training
- Protect Employees from emotional or peer pressure abuse

Boss Role • Mental

Mentally, the role of the Boss is to:

- Prepare and define Employee job descriptions
- Set standards on Employee production
- Set standards for Employee behavior
- Establish clear work objectives and communicate them to Employees
- Supervise and train those who need it
- Clearly define the goals and objectives of the organization
- Correct Employee mistakes
- Hire, discipline, promote, and fire
- Earn the respect of Employees through example rather than fear

Boss Role • Social

Socially, the role of the Boss is to:

- Sponsor social events according to season or holidays
- Establish guidelines and monitor the workplace to protect Employees from sexual harassment
- Monitor the workplace for violations of protocol
- Carry out the goals and objectives of the organization
- Accept responsibility for the performance of others
- Present and administer an objective performance review

Employee Role

The Role of the Employee is to perform the duties for which he/she is responsible. Employees are only accountable for the performance of their own work, whereas the Boss is accountable for the performance of others. The Role of the Employee is to do what the Boss says as long as it applies to fulfilling work objectives.

Employee Role • Physical

Physically, an Employee should:

- Perform assigned tasks and duties
- Show up for work on time
- Dress according to the job requirements
- Stay within physical boundaries

Employee Role • Emotional

Emotionally, an Employee should:

- Support the goals and objectives of the Boss and/or company
- Cooperate with Boss and other Coworkers
- Be enthusiastic
- Not disrupt the workplace

Employee Role • Mental

Mentally, an Employee should:

- Follow the established guidelines for the job
- If allowed, take initiative and be creative
- Be trustworthy and loyal
- Take pride in product work and organization
- Want to learn and grow
- Continue to learn and develop job skills

Employee Role • Social

Socially, an Employee should:

- Attend social functions
- Make an effort to be pleasant and get along
- Participate in group activities

❺ RULES

While there could be layers and layers of Rules for the Boss role, this section will provide some of the basics.

Boss Rules

Boss Rules • Physical

Physically, the Boss should:

- Prepare a written job description that accurately the job duties of the Employee he/she supervises
- Make sure that cleanliness and hygiene are maintained at the workplace
- Ensure that the work environment is safe for Employees at all times
- Write and maintain an accurate organizational chart for the business

Boss Rules • Emotional

Emotionally, the Boss should:

- Keep employees informed about decisions affecting him/her
- Consult employees in matters that affect him/her
- Find out information you need to know from the source
- Not rely on hearsay or second hand information
- Accept Employee mistakes as part of training during the first three months
- Not criticize any of his/her Employees publicly
- Not supervise his/her Employees too closely
- Keep confidences
- Not be jealous of his/her Employee's ability
- Be considerate regarding Employee's personal problems
- Maintain eye contact with his/her Employees during conversations
- Be available to his/her Employees
- Recognize and reward Employees that do good work

Boss Rules • Mental

Mentally, the Boss should:

- Plan and assign work efficiently
- Advise and encourage the advancement of Employees
- Not issue commands without explanation
- Be fair
- Inform Employees of new rules
- Comply with governmental rules
- Not try to be "one of the gang"
- Study records on turnover rate, absenteeism, sick leave, and complaints
- Plan meetings and set the agenda
- Seek information to increase performance

Boss Rules • Social

Socially, the Boss should:

- Make sure that his/her superiors will back up his/her policies
- Not engage in sexual activity with his/her employees
- Be neutral to favors and compliments
- Not discuss personal finances with his/her Employees
- Respect the privacy of his/her Employees
- Fight for the interests of his/her Employee when necessary

Employee Rules

Employee Rules • Physical

Physically, the Employee should:

- Not steal company property
- Arrive at work on time
- Keep honest hours on the job
- Not get the place dirty
- Clean up any mess he/she creates

Employee Rules • Emotional

Emotionally, the Employee should:

- Be willing and cheerful
- Not be too submissive
- Be willing to accept criticism
- Keep confidences
- Not say derogatory things about his/her Boss
- Follow the Boss's instructions
- Maintain sense of own self-esteem
- Not be passive-aggressive regarding work assignments

Employee Rules • Mental

Mentally, the Employee should:

- Ask for clarification when instructions or orders are unclear
- Use initiative when possible
- Put forward and defend your own ideas
- Be willing to take orders
- Give your best effort or quit
- Seek new challenges on the job
- Follow through on work assignments

Employee Rules • Social

Socially, the Employee should:

- Complain to Boss before going to superiors
- Respect his/her Boss's privacy
- Not reveal company secrets
- Attend company functions
- Never criticize his/her Boss publicly

➏ CUSTOMS

Boss Customs • Cultural

Many corporations have established extensive identities that are aspects of the company culture. IBM and Apple Computer are two computer companies that established divergent cultural identities.

As in society itself, the cultural aspects of the relationship may be the dominant factor in the work experience. In some companies and countries "the culture" of the company is so well defined, that people are primarily hired to fit "the culture" as opposed to the aspects or relevant skills or job history in the industry.

Boss Customs • Religious

The distinctions of religion and the workplace are typically separate in Western cultures, however what if your job is in a religious organization? It's unlikely that the Catholic Church is going to hire Protestant ministers.

Perhaps your Boss has a strong belief in a religion which you can't stand for some reason. Even though your religion is not supposed to matter, in this case you may have to participate in a "daily prayer" or something like this which technically isn't part of your job description. However, if you don't, you're fired.

Boss Customs • Political

Politics may or may not be a part of your work culture. If it is, then this is the spot in the HRW evaluation where you list this aspect as it relates to your Boss or Employee for your current job. Perhaps you are a Christian Boss and you don't like it when your Muslim Employees take their prayer break. This would be a good example of a potential Political and Religious cultural conflict, when neither is part of the generic Boss/Employee Relationship.

Employee Customs

Employee Customs • Cultural

Employees may have to subjugate their personal customs to fit in with work environment Customs.

Employee Customs • Political

–

–

Employee Customs • Religious

–

–

Boss/Employee Co-partners

The Environment and Structure alone do not create the Boss/Employee interaction. Two unique and individual Co-partners are required to fill the roles provided by the relationship structure. As always, the Traits, Needs, and Tactics of the individuals playing the Boss and Employee roles form a major part of the experience. Compare your personal situation to the generic traits. The following guidelines are those that apply generically across the board for the Boss/Employee Relationship.

❼ TRAITS

The common perception of the typical Boss might he exemplified by the Dabney Coleman character from the movie Nine to Five. Part of good movie making is to create a horrible character as a Boss, and then have the star of the movie play the Employee who has to outwit the Boss to make sure the movie has a happy ending.

Boss Traits

Boss Traits • Being Attracted

Being Attracted for the Boss means accepting the Employee as a person and being willing to train and advise him/her. If a Boss has some abhorrent dislike of an Employee, then he/she must make special efforts to resolve the situation. If the Boss genuinely likes the personality of an Employee, then this would be a much more comfortable relationship. Unless, of course, the Boss likes an Employee too much, and begins to let personal feelings enter into the generic relationship's structure.

Being Attracted is not to be interpreted in a sexual sense at all. While an Employee may be attractive, or even sexually seductive, the Boss ideally would not allow sexuality to taint the dynamics of the relationship. On the other hand, the dynamics of the Boss as sexual predator of the Employee are so common that the term "sexual harassment" suit have entered the lexicon. Some Employees may even have welcomed such attention if he/she thought it might help them with a promotion or pay raise.

Boss Traits • Being Committed

Being Committed for the Boss means that he/she has a strong desire and commitment to train and motivate the Employee(s) to help the company grow and prosper. This is an important Trait since it reflects his/her willingness to be of service both to the Employee and the company. This trait may require the Boss to juggle issues that often oppose each other. This is because the Boss might have a Boss, and ultimately the Boss is an employee of a company.

Boss Traits • Being Genuine

Being Genuine is the ability of the Boss to be honest and direct about the needs of the business and what is expected of the Employee. This means the Boss will not use subterfuge or questionable tactics to manipulate the Employee. Also, the Boss should not lie or distort work requirements nor ask for impossible feats from an Employee.

Boss Traits • Being Trustworthy

Being Trustworthy reflects such qualities as the Boss's willingness to keep confidences, credit the Employee's paycheck with proper hours, and to support the substance of the Employee's conversations with superiors. This relationship provides many opportunities each day that test this trait. The level of trustworthiness of the Boss is also the benchmark by which the Employees calibrate their level of commitment and trustworthiness to the company.

Boss Traits • Being Emotionally Mature

Being Emotionally Mature is an extremely beneficial trait for a Boss since performance of the role implies responsibility and maturity. Employees must be able to depend on the Boss for motivation and direction while the company depends on the Boss to perform the job duties assigned by the company. If the Boss is mature, he/she will create a much smoother ride on the relationship seesaw.

Boss Traits • Having Communication Skills

Communication Skills are one of the main tools used by a Boss to accomplish his/her many tasks. A Boss must be adept at both the listening and the sending aspects of communication. A Boss must be able to clearly listen and interpret what others are saying as well as be able to explain his/her own position. A Boss who is deficient in this area will create confusion that damages the communication in both directions.

Boss Traits •Having Problem-Solving Skills

Having Problem-Solving Skills is the key to being an effective Boss. Each day many problems will arise at work that require the skillful handling of conflict between parties with different needs. Since the Boss is often ultimately responsible to adjudicate conflicts, he/she must develop the ability to solve problems to a refined level to be successful in this role.

Employee Traits

Resentment of supervision seems to be a universal trait of Employees. If this becomes a problem for the Employee he/she might try to create problems either overtly by "messing up" or covertly through a work "slowdown." On the other hand, Employees often hope to earn a type of approval and acceptance from a Boss or company that only their family or friends can give.

The experience of being an Employee has the potential to create many areas of conflicted feelings.

Employee Traits • Being Attracted

Being Attracted for the Employee is a combination of desire to be working at the job and his/her level of respect for the Boss. The first aspect is fulfilled by being attracted to the type of work, the company itself, or needing money bad enough to work in exchange for money. The second aspect is based on the personal experience the Employee has working for the individual playing the Boss role.

Employee Traits • Being Committed

Being Committed for the Employee is his/her willingness to learn what is required and to do the best possible job with his/her skills. An Employee should consider consciously what level of commitment he/she is willing to give a job.

Employee Traits • Being Genuine

Being Genuine is the ability of the Employee to be honest and sincere on the job. The Employee should be truthful as to his/her abilities and level of job skills. The trait might become an area of personal conflict for example, if "everybody knows" if you tell this Boss your genuine feelings, he/she will fire you on the spot. If you are genuinely genuine, and you are forced to "less than genuine" to keep the only job available to you, most people would understand.

Employee Traits • Being Trustworthy

Being Trustworthy is the degree that the Employee can be trusted by his/her company and Boss. This includes such basics as not stealing, putting accurate hours on time cards, and following through on work assignments. An Employee should be trustworthy for qualities such as showing up for work on time, accepting responsibility for mistakes he/she might make, and not stealing credit for work done by others.

Employee Traits • Being Emotionally Mature

Being Emotionally Mature as an Employee means being responsible and attentive to the personal values that make a good Employee, such as being well-groomed, having pleasant manners, and being willing to pitch in and help. Many employee-style jobs exist and they certainly can be menial and disheartening in many cases. Being Emotionally Mature would be an asset for dealing with these subservient aspects of being an Employee.

Employee Traits •Having Communication Skills

Having Communication Skills as an Employee means being able to communicate with the Boss about projects and job assignments as well as acquiring assertion skills so that he/she is not stepped on. I can say from personal experience that just because you have excellent communication skills, that doesn't mean that you can do anything about it if your Boss is a jerk. I've also heard this occasionally from Employees, so this type of situation is not uncommon.

Its part of the difficulty of this particular relationship, that there seems to be an unwritten rule within the Boss/Employee Relationship that "the Boss is always right" and it's one that Bosses who are jerks take advantage of regularly.

So in this case, your Having Communication Skills could mean that not only are you an excellent listener and able to craft your communications in a third-party-verifiable manner, but that you are able to stay on your side of the seesaw, even if your Boss is standing on your side; all the while keeping a smile on your face.

Employee Traits •Having Problem-Solving Skills

Having Problem-Solving Skills can't be important enough in the Boss/Employee Relationship. By definition a good Boss should have excellent communication skills but this is not always the case.

Theoretically, the Boss should initiate problem-solving for issues that occur in the work place, although an Employee may be in the position of having to communicate a problem to the proper people and initiate problem-solving procedures.

An example might be when an Employee feels that he/she might be being overlooked for advancement and salary increases. In this case it would be a problem for him/her. To solve this situation correctly the Boss would need to find a Win/Win solution that satisfies both the Employee and the Company. Typically, however, it is the Boss's role as defined by the Company, to keep you in your place.

❽ NEEDS

Boss Needs

Boss Needs • Physical

Physically, the Boss needs an Employee who:

- Will perform assigned tasks and duties
- Has the required skill-set and background for job
- Dresses according to the job requirements
- Stays within physical boundaries
- Does not steal company property
- Arrives for work on time
- Keeps honest hours on the job

Boss Needs • Emotional

Emotionally, the Boss needs an Employee who:

- Does not disrupt other employees
- Supports the goals and objectives of the Boss and/or company
- Cooperates with the Boss and other Coworkers
- Is enthusiastic
- Is willing and cheerful
- Is not too submissive
- Is able to accept criticism
- Keeps confidences
- Will not say derogatory things about his/her Boss
- Follows the Boss's instructions and guidelines for job performance

Boss Needs • Mental

Mentally, the Boss needs an Employee who:

- Takes initiative and does the assigned job
- Is trustworthy and loyal
- Takes pride in work product and organization

- Wants to learn and grow
- Continues to learn and develop his/her job skills
- Asks for clarification when instructions or orders are unclear
- Uses initiative when possible
- Puts forward and defends his/her own ideas
- Is willing to take orders
- Gives his/her best effort or quits
- Seeks new challenges on the job
- Follows through on work assignments

Boss Needs • Social

Socially, the Boss needs an Employee who:

- Attends social functions
- Complains to the Boss without going to superiors
- Respects his/her Boss's privacy
- Does not reveal company secrets
- Attends company functions
- Never criticizes his/her Boss publicly

Employee Needs

Employee Needs • Physical

Physically, the Employee needs a Boss who:

- Prepares a written job description that accurately reflects the job duties of the Employees he/she supervises
- Ensures the work environment is safe for the Employees at all times
- Makes sure that cleanliness and hygiene are maintained at the workplace
- Creates a pleasant and productive work environment where his/her Employees can feel good about their work as well as each other

- Trains his/her Employees to the job and establish standards of quality
- Make sure that his/her Employees are paid
- Protects his/her Employees from physical harm

Employee Needs • Emotional

Emotionally, the Employee needs a Boss who:

- Keeps Employees informed about decisions affecting him/her
- Consults Employees in matters that affect him/her
- Finds out information he/she needs to know from the source
- Does not rely on hearsay or second hand information
- Accepts Employee mistakes during training as part of training
- Will not criticize Employees publicly
- Does not supervise Employees to closely
- Can keep confidences
- Is not jealous of Employee's abilities
- Can be considerate regarding the Employee's personal problems
- Maintains eye contact with Employees during conversations
- Is available to Employees
- Recognizes and reward Employees for work well done
- Supports Employees emotionally in regards to work objectives
- Inspires Employees through example
- Earns the respect of Employees through example rather than fear
- Protects Employees from emotional harm
- Doesn't make the Employee feel like everyday at work could be their last

Employee Needs • Mental

Mentally, the Employee needs a Boss who:

- Writes and maintains an accurate job duties description for the position
- Plans and assigns work efficiently
- Advises and encourages the advancement of opportunities
- Does not issue commands without explanation
- Is fair
- Informs Employees of new rules
- Complies with governmental rules
- Doesn't try to be "one of the gang"
- Studies records on turnover rates, absenteeism, sick leave, and complaints
- Plans meetings and sets the agenda
- Prepares and defines his/her Employee's job descriptions
- Sets standards on Employee production
- Sets standards for Employee behavior
- Establishes clear work objectives and communicates them clearly to Employees
- Supervises and trains those who need it
- Clearly defines the goals and objectives of the organization
- Corrects the mistakes of his/her Employees by demonstrating the correct procedures

Employee Needs • Social

Socially, the Employee needs a Boss who:

- Doesn't engage in sexual activity with Employees
- Is neutral to favors and compliments
- Does not discuss personal finances with Employees
- Respects the privacy of Employees
- Fights for the interests of his/her Employee when necessary
- Sponsors social events according to season or holidays

- Does not allow Employees or others to interject sexual overtones into the work place
- Polices the work place for violations of protocol
- Carries out the goals and objectives of the organization
- Accepts responsibility for the performance of others
- Presents and administers an objective performance review

❾ TACTICS

Boss Tactics

Boss Tactics • Positive

Some positive tactics of the Boss Role are:

- To follow the generic rules of being a Boss
- To remember when he/she was an Employee and what that felt like
- To be honest and fair with all Employees, not showing any favoritism
- To ask questions before giving orders
- To seek both sides of the story when there is Employee conflicts
- To hold meetings where he/she asks if there is anything that he/she can do for the Employees
- To train from a competent manual using it as a third-party
- To addresses problem Employees in private, not in front of the public or other Employees
- Lead by example not fear
- To strive to create a positive PEMS Environment for the Employees given the realities of the work itself

Boss Tactics • Negative

We could start by reversing all the positive tactics listed above. Every Boss/Employee is so different that the nuances of positive vs. negative Tactics could go on for some pages.

One particularly popular form of using negative tactics in the Boss Role is using the power of his/her role to create:

- Fear
- Power
- Force
- Manipulation

And yet, there is probably someone out there with a book and a seminar that will say, "Fear, power, force and manipulation are the most positive tactics for a Boss because it's the only way you will get any work accomplished."

If you understand the HRW analogy of relationships, particularly the seesaw idea, you would understand that the most effective strategy to get the most action out of any relationship is to have positive Traits and to use positive Tactics from whatever side of the seesaw you find yourself on.

If this is not followed, although there may be some short gains for a Company using rape and pillage methods, this does not come free and people and the Environment get hurt in the process.

Employee Tactics

Tactics of the upset Employee are certainly the essence for many movies in the movie-making world. I would wager that just about everyone would have two or three good stories like this.

Part of the problem is that Employees are often seen as powerless and they just have to put up with a negative Boss or lose their job. Many examples also exist where the Employees *did* have positive traits and *were* using positive Tactics but that had no bearing on the way they were treated by their Boss(s).

So, what's an Employee to do? I would suggest staying true to yourself and doing your best to survive in a hostile environment in case you find yourself there. If you are one of the lucky Employees who do have your dream job, Boss, and everything nice, then I congratulate you. It's very possible.

Employee Tactics • Positive

Some positive tactics of the Employee Role are:

- Following the PEMS Roles and Rules as described in HRW
- Asking other Employees how they deal with the Boss
- Counting to ten if you are a short-tempered person
- Not letting Boss problems getting to you and/or leaving that job as soon as is practical

Employee Tactics • Negative

Some negative tactics of the Employee Role are:

- Not following any of the PEMS Employee guidelines
- Avoiding work through a deliberate slowdown
- Making mistakes on purpose just to irritate the Boss
- Using personal connection to the Boss for your own gain or to achieve status over other Coworkers
- Encouraging elicit conduct for personal gain or ego satisfaction

CHAPTER 18

*T*he Coworker/Coworker Relationship

Welcome to the world of the Coworker/Coworker Relationship. This is a relationship that many people don't give much thought or consideration to, yet many people are more heavily involved in Coworker/Coworker Relationships than all the rest of their relationships combined.

Coworkers present a special HRW situation in that you may be forced to work with people that you don't like and can't do anything about. As a result, you may find yourself expected to maintain social graces with others even though this may have no direct bearing on your job duties.

Coworker/Coworker Environment

Other than the classic aspects of Location, Timing, and Duration such as listed in the Boss/Employee Relationship, various other factors can be part of the Coworker/Coworker Environment:

- Cleanliness of the Coworker
- Quality of the Coworker's personality
- How involved you must be with the Coworker to perform your job
- The Coworker's job morale

Personal factors that can impact you about the Environment are:

- Clothes you must wear to "compete" with Coworkers
- The type of people who make up your Coworkers

❶ LOCATION

The location of the Coworker/Coworker Relationship is wherever you work together with other Coworkers. This may include any set of circumstances. You may be in a rock band, working on the subway, or typing for an insurance company.

❷ DURATION

Duration is how long you and your Coworker have been working together at that job. Perhaps you've both been at the company for 10 years, but you just started working in the same office 6 months ago. Maybe you are both teachers, and now you are teaching at the same primary school.

❸ TIMING

Timing is the amount of minutes and/or hours and time of day you spend interacting with your Co-partner. This is separate from activities such as simply sitting next to each other answering the phone all day.

Coworker Timing would involve when you are working or socializing directly with each other. For example, you might go to lunch together, or have a meeting where you are working together on a project. Perhaps this person is your liaison from another office, and you send reports back and forth.

Think of your interactions with each person you work with. If they involve a work purpose or a social exchange, these would be the Timings for your Coworker/Coworker Relationship.

Coworker/Coworker Structure

Because of the time typically spent at work (30-60 hours a week) many Coworkers have a built in system for camaraderie. They share multiple daily events at the work place that outsiders aren't privy to. They hear and share company secrets and gossip, punching out for each other, and taking long lunches. On the other hand, Coworkers may be competitive, difficult to work with, or even try to sabotage you for reasons only he/she understands.

On the good side, friendly Coworkers are a positive source of satisfaction. If your work is difficult to bear, yet your Coworkers make it fun or worthwhile, then for many people, this takes precedence over pay, opportunity, security, and/or challenge.

❹ ROLES

You might think that the role of the Coworker is to do his/her job. But those job duties take place under the Boss/Employee Relationship. When you think about it, the true role in the Coworker/Coworker Relationship is simply to get along with the other Coworkers.

Even if the Coworkers are specifically required to work interactively to get a job done (professional team sports, actors and directors) they are working together to perform certain duties and thus expected to get along. These factors turn the role description of the Coworker towards aspects of public relations and office politics, which is an area that many people can get into trouble without realizing it.

Another area of confusion for many people is becoming friends with Coworkers. When people leave school, they lose their built-in social system. Work then becomes their social outlet by default.

What happens is that many people want Coworker/Coworker Relationships to be played by the rules of the Friend/Friend Relationships. This causes many problems and basic confusions for the person who doesn't know HRW.

Can a Coworker become a friend? It's not that it's impossible, improbable is more like it. Think of it this way. If your current Coworker (who is a great "friend") no longer worked at your company, would you still be as close with your Coworker/friend? Not only from your side, but also from his/her side as well?

The first and best test of the "Coworker/friend" question is whether or not you were friends with this person before you started working with them. If yes, they are probably a friend (who got you the job) if not, they are a Coworker (and he/she wouldn't maintain the friendship if you left.) The problem being is that if you felt a person was a friend, but they never talked to you again, you would feel hurt. However, a Coworker would by default never talk to you again, ever.

There is a contrasting dynamic to this as well. Let's assume you would never even remotely want to be friends with a particular Coworker. If you do work with this person you are more or less obligated to be as friendly and professional in your association as possible. This is something you would never do if you didn't work together.

If you did become friends with a Coworker, your relationship would eventually be governed by the rules of the Friend/Friend Relationship, but this is exceedingly rare.

Coworker Roles

Coworker Roles • Physical

Physically, the role of the Coworker is to:

- Be accountable for the performance of own work
- Take care of own work space and responsibilities
- Returned borrowed work items
- Repay debts and favors

Coworker Roles • Emotional

Emotionally, the role of the Coworker is to:

- Be a pleasant person with whom to work
- Don't be emotionally needy
- Don't volunteer too many details about your personal life

Coworker Roles • Mental

Mentally, the role of the Coworker is to:

- Be respectful and pleasantly neutral to other Coworkers
- Help other Coworkers if they request it
- Ask for help with job duties if you don't understand something
- Not dig for personal details about a Coworkers personal life

Coworker Roles • Social

Socially, the role of the Coworker is to:

- Participate in social functions organized by work
- Contribute toward gifts for your Coworkers
- Be friendly but somewhat distant

❺ RULES

The rules of Coworker/Coworker Relationships need to be customized for your specific working environment. For example, a list of Coworker rules that must be followed would certainly be longer if you worked for IBM rather than a two-person real estate office. In bigger companies, you might be given a list of "guidelines" that effectively tell you the rules you must follow.

Think of the listings that follow as general guidelines. Adapt them to your own Coworker/Coworker situations. In some work situations, you may be stuck with a person you couldn't warm up to even if you were cremated together. In this situation there are special rules that apply to the Coworker/Coworker Relationship.

Coworker Rules

Coworker Rules • Physical

Physically, the Coworker/Coworker Rules are to:

- Be cooperative with regard to shared physical working conditions
- Be willing to help when requested
- Don't hoard supplies from fellow Coworkers

Physically, if you can't get along with a Coworker:

- Try to organize your work space and schedule so you have as little face-to-face contact as possible

Coworker Rules • Emotional

Emotionally, the rules of the Coworker/Coworker Relationship are:

- Maintain a willing and cheerful attitude
- Not be too submissive
- Be willing to accept criticism
- Keep confidences
- Address his/her Coworker by his/her first name
- Not complain to superiors under normal circumstances
- Ask for help and advice when necessary
- Not be nosy about your Coworker's private lives

Emotionally, if you can't get along with your Coworker:

- Work cooperatively despite feelings of animosity
- Confront, don't ignore, a conflict situation
- Be polite and friendly with the person
- Don't talk about him/her behind his hack
- Strive to be fair in relations with one another
- Don't invite his/her to family celebrations
- Don't pointedly ignore the Coworker
- Don't display hypocritical affection for the Coworker

Coworker Rules • Mental

Mentally, the Rules of the Coworker/Coworker Relationship are to:

- Seek clarification when job descriptions or assignments are unclear
- Use initiative where possible
- Put forward and defend your own ideas
- Respect your Coworker's personal privacy

Mentally, if you can't get along with a Coworker:

- Attempt to recall if you've said or done anything that might have offended the Coworker
- Clarify your thoughts, feelings, and needs before communicating with your Coworker
- Calmly speak to the Coworker in private if you hear that he/she is saying things behind your back
- Respect each other's privacy
- Don't discuss what is said in confidence
- Be honest but careful about comments
- Don't reveal intimate details of your personal life
- Don't discuss details of your life outside your work
- Don't push too hard to turn an enemy into a friend
- Stay on your side of the seesaw
- Take action (communicate) if someone keeps wandering over to your side of the seesaw.

Coworker Rules • Social

Socially, the rules of the Coworker/Coworker Relationship are:

- Offer assistance if needed or requested
- Adhere to company guidelines or culture for interaction

⑥ CUSTOMS

Think of where you work as a mini culture, religion and political system all in one. In many larger companies, this is exactly the situation you face. So, when thinking of the following areas governed by your work, see if there are any "customs" that are as much a part of your work demands as the company roles and rules.

For example, in many ad agencies and Hollywood type jobs, you may be hired as 9 to 5, but if you don't get there early and go to some work-related function every night, you won't be working there long.

Company customs depend on the cultural, religious, and political aspects of the company and its founding leaders. I could name some names here and you would instantly conjure up what it would be like working for this man or woman.

In this increasingly multi-cultural society, you may find yourself working with someone from an entirely foreign culture than your own. You may have to be extra careful not to offend a Coworker by unknowingly disrespecting their culture. Perhaps where you work you are the odd person and every Coworker is a different race, religion, or country from you. Now the pressure will be on you to conform to their Customs of which you may be unsure.

Coworker Customs• Cultural

Respect cultural icons of a person if unique or different from your own.

Coworker Customs • Religious

If a person is a serious adherent to a religion, give that person respect for following their beliefs.

Coworker Customs• Political

Allow a person to express and defend their own political beliefs without rancor.

Coworker/Coworker Co-partners

❼ TRAITS

Coworker Traits

Personality traits are the biggest key to liking a person you work with. If you like his/her traits, you will like them as a person. Getting to know a person at work is one way of learning about their traits, at least as they exhibit them at the job.

You can also be sure that most people present a more "professional side" to their personality at work, and if you knew them on a personal basis, they might be less appealing. Following are the HRW breakdown of HRW traits as they relate to the Coworker/Coworker Relationship.

Coworker Traits • Being Attracted

Being Attracted in the Coworker/Coworker Relationship is not mandatory for a working relationship. If you are attracted (because he/she is a nice person) your job will be more pleasant to perform.

In fact, you are more likely to find yourself in a Coworker/Coworker Relationship with someone you hate and would never hang around with on your free time. In this situation, your goal is to be as sociable as possible under the circumstances.

Special Point:

Being Attracted sexually to a Coworker is always a troublesome area. Even if both are single, available, and there is no company policy against the practice, initiating a romantic or sexual relationship with a Coworker always has a more complicated downside than might appear during the first glow of sexual attraction.

The worst possibility would be after a personal or sexual relationship has gone cold, then having to see or interact with that person for the rest of your days at that job. If it's happened to you, you know already it's not pretty.

Sexual Attraction is always a potential problem in the work environment because working intensely and in close proximity for many hours can bring on sexual feelings that would never bloom otherwise between the two people.

Also, being required to attend "work meetings" or going away for "work seminars" provides the Environmental means and opportunity for attraction to take place which, let's face it, doesn't happen much in "real life."

Coworker Traits • Being Committed

Being Committed involves performing your job with professionalism within the context of a Coworker/Coworker Relationship. By virtue of working at your job together, you will have a natural commitment to the Coworkers in your company as opposed to outsiders.

In today's work environment companies via their mangers often try to build "teams" and pump up the volume on working together, blah, blah. They do this because they don't actually know How Relationships Work so they inject artificiality into the mix to make themselves feel like they are doing something. The Coworker/Coworker Relationship has weak bonds already, so trying to falsely make everybody function as a team by playing some games on the weekend is degrading to the Coworker.

Some jobs though do require commitment between Coworkers, such as working on an oil rig, or being a soldier, or an astronaut. In these situations training is intense and ongoing as it is required to create the trust and build the teamwork for Being Committed.

Coworker Traits • Being Genuine

Being Genuine is important. You should never pretend you like a person if you feel just the opposite. Your job in this situation is to simply do your work and be pleasant and neutral. If you do like your Coworkers, you will find it easy to be genuine.

On the other hand, you'd be advised not to reveal your deepest darkest feelings, or make comments in the heat of the moment that you might find yourself sorry for later. And you might not want to show everyone how smart you are on your first day at a new job. Your genius might be misinterpreted by your new coworkers.

Coworker Traits • Being Trustworthy

It is important to keep confidences that are shared under the common bond of being an employee. However, Being Trustworthy is difficult to maintain as a Coworker. There are built-in conflicts of interest with the Boss/Employee Relationship.

For example, if two Coworkers are conspiring to cheat on their hours, they may expect you to be trustworthy and not tell the Boss. However, this conflicts directly with your responsibility to be trustworthy to the Boss. If you tell your Boss, you will be "right," but your Coworkers could then make your daily working environment a living hell.

Coworker Traits • Being Emotionally Mature

Being Emotionally Mature will improve your chances of enjoying your job. You will be able to realistically judge the value of what you do and adjust it to your goals and needs. With respect to your Coworkers, it will also help you cope with the typical ups and downs of petty office politics.

Coworker Traits • Having Communication Skills

Having Communication Skills will enable you to work more easily with your Coworkers. Many times communication can be misunderstood. Thus, watching for the classic patterns and requesting clarification at the appropriate times will help to avoid the many potential communication problems that can occur between Coworkers.

Coworker Traits • Having Problem-Solving Skills

Problems will inevitably occur in any pressure-packed work environment. Having the skills to resolve conflict will help you make the environment of your work place as friction free as possible. One good aspect is that many companies do provide training on communications principles and problem-solving skills in some form.

❸ NEEDS

Needs in this relationship are typically associated with getting the job done. For many people, the Coworker/Coworker Relationship is the major way they fulfill social needs. Their identity as a worker is the only identity they have.

Coworker Needs

Following are the HRW breakdown of Needs as they relate to the Coworker/Coworker Relationship.

Coworker Needs • Physical

Physically, the needs of the Coworker are to:

- Enjoy safe and healthy physical working conditions
- Have the equipment and supplies he/she needs to perform job duties
- Not be bothered or disturbed while doing their work

Coworker Needs • Emotional

Emotionally, the needs of the Coworker are to:

- Enjoy the emotional working environment
- Feel emotionally safe
- Be given respect as a person
- Maintain civil exchanges with Coworkers
- Be able to ask for help and advice when necessary
- Be able to keep emotional life and personal problems private
- Not pry into the personal lives of Coworkers

Coworker Needs • Mental

Mentally, the needs of the Coworker are to:

– Be properly trained for their specific job
– Seek clarification when job descriptions or assignments are unclear
– Be able to contribute own ideas and talents
– Be able to work on own initiative where possible
– Enjoy the respect and admiration of other Coworkers

Coworker Needs • Social

Socially, the needs of the Coworker are to:

– Be free to ask assistance if needed or requested
– Not do work assigned to other Coworkers
– Accept his/her fair share of the work load
– Not engage in sexual activity with other Coworkers
– Not be competitive with fellow Coworkers
– Be a cooperative team member
– Be supportive of Coworkers not present
– Not criticize other Coworkers publicly
– Repay debts, favors, and compliments
– Not feel free to take up as much of the other's time as one desires

❾ TACTICS

Remember that tactics are ways and means that a person uses to meet his/her needs. If you are the recipient of strange tactics from Coworkers that don't seem to be aligned with any purpose at work, think back to the needs that person might have on a personal level (based on his/her traits). Experiencing negative Tactics "out of the blue" from Coworkers is not a good sign.

Coworker Tactics • Positive

Some positive tactics of the Coworker Relationship are:

- Make a special effort to make new Coworkers feel comfortable
- Be genuine with the Coworker
- Offer assistance if needed or requested
- Don't do work assigned to other Coworkers
- Accept your fair share of the work load
- Don't engage in sexual activity with other Coworkers
- Don't compete with fellow Coworkers
- Do cooperate with other team members
- Be supportive of Coworker not present
- Don't criticize other Coworkers publicly
- Repay debts, favors, and compliments
- Don't feel free to take up as much of the other's time as one desires

Coworker Tactics • Negative

Some negative tactics of the Coworker/Coworker Relationship are:

- Not offering assistance if needed or requested
- Not accepting your fair share of the work load
- Sexual innuendo or conversational foreplay
- Engaging in sexual activity with other Coworkers
- Competing with fellow Coworkers
- Not cooperating with other team members
- Criticizing Coworkers not present
- Criticizing other Coworkers publicly
- Not repaying debts, favors, and compliments
- Feeling free to take up as much of the other's time as one desire
- Discussing Coworker conflicts with customers or in public

*P*art *T*hree: Intro

Part Three provides a simple, yet extremely effective 3-step system to evaluate any personal relationship.

If you follow these steps in order, you will be well rewarded for your efforts.

CHAPTER 21

*P*ractical: HRW

Evaluating Your Personal Relationships

How Relationships Work presents an objective 3-step system that can be used to analyze and evaluate your personal versions of the 12 classic "generic" human relationships as described in Part Two. Once you learn this system your questions and issues with relationships will be easily answered and clearly understood. As you become familiar with this method of analysis, you will gain an ever deeper understanding of the dynamics of all your personal relationships.

This system is easy to follow and understand but you will have to commit to studying and applying the principles of HRW to your personal relationships.

Part One brought you into the system and describes how the three elements of a relationship are put together.

Part Two describes each generic relationship broken down into its 9 specific sub-parts. Once you know the ideal patterns of the generic relationships, you can compare them to the specifics of your personal relationships.

Take the generic Boss/Employee relationship. All Bosses have generic roles and rules that fit the role of the Boss. All Employees have certain duties and responsibilities that fit the role of the Employee.

Using this book you can compare the ideal Boss/Employee Relationship to your personal experience of a Boss/Employee Relationship. If you like you could evaluate any Boss/Employee tionship you've ever had.

Are you, the Boss, acting how a generic Boss should act? Are your Employees following their roles as ideally as they should? If you are the Employee is there anything unusual about your Boss? Are there some "stranger than fiction" aspects to your Employee experience?

Once you know the generic structure of a relationship, you can analyze any personal relationship. If your personal relationship follows the generic structure, it is positive. If it strays from the generic structure, it is negative.

What You Need to Know Before Going Any Further

This evaluation system only takes three steps, but they are not necessarily easy. I have spent many years teaching Self-Parenting students How Relationships Work. The main thing I have learned from this experience is that anyone can read the material and understand what they read. But as soon as I take the book away and ask some basic questions, I typically get a blank stare and a few low mumbles.

To truly understand and use this system, you must be able to recall the system's terminology without reading the book. This is actually Step One of the system, and very important.

You can use a cheat sheet while you are learning; hopefully you won't need it for long. The questions you need to know the answers to are on the next page.

Step Two is to put each of your personal Co-partners on their respective sides of the various seesaws that you are on.

Many times this alone is clarifying enough to put some of the problems you are having into perspective. Once you have done this, you can take any relationship and investigate it further by using the forms in this book and going to the related chapter.

That would be Step Three and the reason for this book.

CHAPTER 22

Step 1: Learning HRW Terminology

The purpose of this section is for you to perform some practical "lab work" to more fully appreciate How Relationships Work. If you are unable to answer the following questions clearly and without the book, then you are going to find it very difficult to truly understand How Relationships Work. If you are serious about learning the HRW System, you need to be able to answer the following:

A Single Relationship

- How does a relationship work?
- What are the three elements of any relationship?
- What are the three parts used to evaluate the first element.
- What are the three parts used to evaluate the second element.
- What are the three parts used to evaluate the third element.

The Twelve Generic Human Relationships

- What are the three types of human relationships?
- How many categories does the first type have and what are they?
- How many categories does the second type have and what are they?
- How many categories does the third type have, and what are they?

What You Need to Know Before Going Any Further

You need to be able to answer the prior basic questions without the book.

If you know what PEMS means and can name the 7 Traits of the HRW Co-partner, you get bonus points.

PEMS means:

–

–

–

–

The Seven Traits of HRW are:

–

–

–

–

–

–

–

CHAPTER 23

Step 2: Listing Your Relationships

The next practical step of HRW is to list all your Co-partners in their respective and proper relational structures. As often as not, the clarity of having the right Co-partner on the right relational seesaw, solves many problems that my clients have.

In actual fact, once a client defines what relationship structure is involved, and which element contains their problem area, he/she typically knows already what to do. They just want to get back to their relationship and take the steps needed to fix it.

Please see/hear/feel me when I say, creating this list is important. This is a very "real world" exercise. It represents the first time you begin to place your personal circumstances into its generic equivalent.

Listing Your Primary Family Relationships

Your Primary Parent/Child Relationships (As the Child)

Your Parent (Mother) Child (You)

_____/_____

Your Parent (Father) Child (You)

_____/_____

Sibling/Sibling Relationships (You as the Sibling)

If you have brothers or sisters, name your Co-partners.

You Sibling

_____/_____

You Sibling

_____/_____

You Sibling

_____/_____

You Sibling

_____/_____

You Sibling

_____/_____

Your Children

If you have children, name your Co-partners.

Parent (You) Child

_____/_____

Parent (You) Child

_____/_____

Parent (You) Child

_____/_____

Parent (You) Child

_____/_____

Parent (You) Child

Grandparent/Grandchild Relationship

If you are a grandparent, then name your Co-partners.

You   Grandchild
_____/_____

You   Grandchild
_____/_____

You   Grandchild
_____/_____

You   Grandchild
_____/_____

You   Grandchild
_____/_____

You   Grandchild
_____/_____

You   Grandchild
_____/_____

You   Grandchild
_____/_____

You   Grandchild
_____/_____

You   Grandchild
_____/_____

Adult Child/Aging Parent Relationship

If you are over 50 year's old and your parents are still alive, then name your Co-partners.

Adult Child (You)   Aging Mother   (Age)
_____/_____   _____

Adult Child (You)   Aging Father)   (Age)
_____/_____   _____

Listing Your Maternal Family Relationships

Maternal Grandparent/Grandchild Relationship

If your mother's parents are alive, then name your Co-partners.

Maternal Grandmother   You

_____/_____

Maternal Grandfather   You

_____/_____

Maternal Aunt/Uncle Relationships

If your mother has Brothers and/or Sisters, then name your Co-partners.

Mother's Siblings   You

_____/_____

Mother's Siblings   You

_____/_____

Mother's Siblings   You

_____/_____

Mother's Siblings   You

_____/_____

Mother's Siblings   You

_____/_____

Mother's Siblings   You

_____/_____

Mother's Siblings   You

_____/_____

Mother's Siblings   You

_____/_____

Mother's Siblings   You

_____/_____

Maternal Cousins Relationships

If your mother's brothers and/or sisters have children, they are your First Cousins

Aunt/Uncle Child	You
_____/_____	

Aunt/Uncle Child	You
_____/_____	

Aunt/Uncle Child	You
_____/_____	

Aunt/Uncle Child	You
_____/_____	

Aunt/Uncle Child	You
_____/_____	

Aunt/Uncle Child	You
_____/_____	

Aunt/Uncle Child	You
_____/_____	

Aunt/Uncle Child	You
_____/_____	

Aunt/Uncle Child	You
_____/_____	

Aunt/Uncle Child	You
_____/_____	

Aunt/Uncle Child	You
_____/_____	

Aunt/Uncle Child	You
_____/_____	

Aunt/Uncle Child	You
_____/_____	

Aunt/Uncle Child	You
_____/_____	

Aunt/Uncle Child	You
_____/_____	

Listing Your Paternal Family Relationships

Paternal Grandparent/Grandchild Relationship

If your father's parents are alive, then name your Co-partners.

Paternal Grandmother   You

_____/_____

Paternal Grandfather   You

_____/_____

Paternal Aunt/Uncle Relationships

If your father has Brothers and/or Sisters, then name your Co-partners.

Father's Siblings   You

_____/_____

Father's Siblings   You

_____/_____

Father's Siblings   You

_____/_____

Father's Siblings   You

_____/_____

Father's Siblings   You

_____/_____

Father's Siblings   You

_____/_____

Father's Siblings   You

_____/_____

Father's Siblings   You

_____/_____

Father's Siblings   You

_____/_____

Paternal Cousins Relationships

If your father's brothers and/or sisters have children, they are your Cousins

Aunt/Uncle Child   You

_____/_____

Aunt/Uncle Child   You

_____/_____

Aunt/Uncle Child   You

_____/_____

Aunt/Uncle Child   You

_____/_____

Aunt/Uncle Child   You

_____/_____

Aunt/Uncle Child   You

_____/_____

Aunt/Uncle Child   You

_____/_____

Aunt/Uncle Child   You

_____/_____

Aunt/Uncle Child   You

_____/_____

Aunt/Uncle Child   You

_____/_____

Aunt/Uncle Child   You

_____/_____

Aunt/Uncle Child   You

_____/_____

Aunt/Uncle Child   You

_____/_____

Aunt/Uncle Child   You

_____/_____

Aunt/Uncle Child   You

_____/_____

Listing Your Social Relationships

One thing I typically find when consulting is that many people believe they have more friends then they actually do. Once you stop calling everyone you know a friend, and start giving them the role that represents your truest relationship, many people often find they have no friends at all.

Friend/Friend (True Friends) Relationships

Best Friend   You

_____/_____

Second Best Friend   You

_____/_____

Third Best Friend   You

_____/_____

Friend/Friend (Acquaintances) Relationships

Acquaintance   You

_____/_____

Acquaintance   You

_____/_____

Acquaintance   You

_____/_____

Acquaintance   You

_____/_____

Acquaintance   You

_____/_____

Acquaintance   You

_____/_____

Acquaintance   You

_____/_____

Your Boyfriend/Girlfriend Relationship (Three Potential Stages)

Dating Partner/Dating Partner

Dating Partner   Dating Partner

_____/_____

Dating Partner   Dating Partner

_____/_____

Dating Partner   Dating Partner

_____/_____

Boyfriend/Girlfriend

Boyfriend   Girlfriend

_____/_____

Fiancé/Fiancée

Fiancé   Fiancée

_____/_____

Your Husband/Wife Relationship

Husband   Wife

_____/_____

Ex-Husband/Ex-Wife Relationship

Ex-Husband   Ex-Wife

_____/_____

Ex-Husband   Ex-Wife

_____/_____

Your In-law/In-law Relationships

Mother-In-Law   You

_____/_____

Father-In-Law   You

_____/_____

Sibling-In-Law   You

_____/_____

Sibling-In-Law   You

_____/_____

Sibling-In-Law   You

_____/_____

Sibling-In-Law   You

_____/_____

Sibling-In-Law   You

_____/_____

Sibling-In-Law   You

_____/_____

Sibling-In-Law   You

_____/_____

Your Neighbor/Neighbor Relationship

Closest Neighbor   You

_____/_____

Next Closest   You

_____/_____

Next Closest   You

_____/_____

Next Closest   You

_____/_____

Next Closest   You

_____/_____

Next Closest   You

_____/_____

Listing Your Work Relationships

Boss/Employee Relationship

Are you the Boss with Employees?

Boss (You)   Employee

_____/_____

Boss (You)   Employee

_____/_____

Boss (You)   Employee

_____/_____

Boss (You)   Employee

_____/_____

Your Boss/Employee Relationship

Are you an Employee?

Boss   Employee (You)

_____/_____

Boss   Employee (You)

_____/_____

Your Coworker/Coworker Relationship

Do you have Coworkers at your job?

Coworker   You

_____/_____

Coworker   You

_____/_____

Coworker   You

_____/_____

Coworker   You

_____/_____

Coworker   You

_____/_____

CHAPTER 24

*S*tep 3: *Evaluating Any Relationship*

Personal Relationship Evaluation

It turns out that there are 27 slots where the specific details of your personal relationships can go. Use each section to note specifics of the relationship you are evaluating. It's especially for the specifics of your relationship that aren't in the book.

_____ / _____ Relationship.

The ENVIRONMENT: Positive, Negative, or Neutral Factors:	
Location	
Duration	
Timing	

The Seesaw Structure (One Side)		Role A
Role A	Physical	
	Emotional	
	Mental	
	Social	
Rules A	Physical	
	Emotional	

Rules A (cont.)	Mental	
	Social	
Customs A	Cultural	
	Religious	
	Political	

The Seesaw Structure (The Other Side)		Role B
Role B	Physical	
	Emotional	
	Mental	
	Social	
Rules B	Physical	
	Emotional	

Rules B (cont.)	Mental	
	Social	
Customs B	Cultural	
	Religious	
	Political	

The Two Co-partners		Co-partner A: _____
Traits A	Is Attracted	
	Is Committed	
	Is Genuine	
	Is Trustworthy	
	Is Mature	
	Has Communication Skills	
	Has Problem Solving Skills	

Needs A	Physical	
	Emotional	
	Mental	
	Social	
Tactics A	Positive	
	Negative	

The Two Co-partners		Co-partner B: _____
Traits B	Is Attracted	
	Is Committed	
	Is Genuine	
	Is Trustworthy	
	Is Mature	
	Has Commu- nication Skills	
	Has Problem Solving Skills	

Needs B	Physical	
	Emotional	
	Mental	
	Social	
Tactics B	Positive	
	Negative	

CHAPTER 25

Questions to Ask Yourself

Once you have read through the chapter related to your personal relationship and have made some notes, here are some questions to ask yourself:

Within an ENVIRONMENT: Location

- Is the Environment positive, negative, or neutral?
- Is there anything unusual about the Environment?
- Is the Environment particularly supportive?
- Is the Location the only reason for the relationship?
- Is the Environment in or out of your control?
- Is the Environment particularly harsh?
- Does the Environment favor one Co-partner over the other?
- Is everybody happy with the Environment?
- Does the Environment affect both Co-partners equally?
- Does the Environment separate the Co-partners in any way?
- Does the Environment bind the Co-partners in any way?
- Is the Environment not a major factor in your relationship?
- Does the weather, such as heat, cold, or moisture affect one Co-partner more than the other?

Duration

- How is the Duration working for you so far?
- Are you worried about the Duration ending anytime soon?
- Is your Co-partner content with its current progress as far as Duratioon is concerned?
- Are you thinking too far ahead in your relationship?
- Is there anything interesting about the Duration?

Timing

- Is the number of times you interact per day/week appropriate for your relationship?
- Are you happy with the number of times that you interact?
- Are you happy about the time of day you interact?
- Are you happy with the number of times you see your Co-partner?
- Is your Co-partner happy with the number of times you interact?
- Does the Environment have any bearing or affect the number of times you interact?
- Does the time of day affect this relationship in any way?
- Does this relationship always take place at the same time?
- Does this relationship have anything to do with the Internet?
- Is there anything unusual about the time of day or number of times you interact?

On a Seesaw STRUCTURE:

Here are some questions to jog the Structure issues.

Roles

- Is your relationship clearly one of the 12 generic relationships?
- Are you on the correct seesaw with your Co-partner?
- Are you and your Co-partner both on the same seesaw?
- Is your Co-partner on a similar seesaw with anyone else?
- Do you and your Co-partner share more than one seesaw structure? If so, what are they and how many are there?
- Does this seesaw have any elements of a professional relationship?
- Is this structure dependant on money to exist?
- Is this structure defined by a specific service?
- Is this structure provided primarily by the government?
- Does your Role feel like it's something other than its stated purpose?
- Does it feel like both Roles are being followed physically?
- Does it feel like both Roles are being followed emotionally?
- Does it feel like both Roles are being followed mentally?
- Does it feel like both Roles are being followed socially

Rules

- Do the Rules being followed seem consistent?
- Are there any odd rules to your relationship?
- Is there any disparity between knowing the rules and following the rules?
- Are any Physical Rules being broken by your or your Co-partner?

- Are any Emotional Rules being broken by your or your Co-partner?
- Are any Mental Rules being broken by your or your Co-partner?
- Are any Social Rules being broken by your or your Co-partner?
- Have you ever discussed relationship rules with your Co-partner?
- Are there any "missing" rules?
- Are there any "extra" rules?

Customs

- Is your Co-partner from a different cultural, religious, or political system?
- Are there any language differences or communication difficulties?
- Did your Co-partner grow up in a different county?
- Is there anything about your ages or roles about which your culture would disapprove or find unusual?
- Are there any religious practices or customs of particular importance to you or your Co-partner?
- Is politics a factor in any way as far as your relationship is concerned?
- Does your country of origin differ from your Co-partner?
- Are there any extreme differences in social upbringing or financial status?
- Is poverty or extreme wealth a factor in this relationship?
- Are the Co-partners strongly united by a specific cultural, religious, or political system different to "the norm?"
- Does you Copartner seem like he/she is from another planet?

Between TWO CO-PARTNERS: Traits

Here are some questions to jog the Co-partner issues.

- Is your Co-partner a good person or a bad person?
- Is your Co-partner a mean person or a nice person?
- Do you like your Co-partner?
- Does your Co-partner like you?
- What do your friends say about your Co-partner?
- Does your Co-partner enjoy positive relationships with others?
- As Co-partners do you both seem equally attracted?
- Has anyone commented on you attractions being different?
- Does you Co-partner have something about them that everyone likes?
- Are you attracted to your Co-partner for reasons other than the specific seesaw you are on?
- Is one Co-partner more attracted than the other?
- Are both Co-partners equally committed?
- Is one Co-partner more committed than the other?
- Are both Co-partners equally genuine?
- Are both Co-partners equally trustworthy?
- Are the Co-partners relatively the same in emotionally maturity?
- Do both Co-partners have communication skills?
- Are both Co-partners compatible communication wise?
- Do both Co-partners have problem-solving skills?
- Is one Co-partner more of a problem-solver then the other?
- Does either Co-partner shy away from problem-solving or make it difficult?

Needs

- Are you and your Co-partner putting in equal amounts of energy on your seesaw?
- Is your Co-partner working at all on his/her side of the seesaw?
- Is your Co-partner too busy to be on his/her side of the seesaw?
- Are you attracted to your Co-partner because of his/her role on a professional seesaw?
- Do both Co-partners agree they are on the same category of relationship seesaw?
- Is there anything about this Co-partner that seems similar to other Co-partners you've experienced?
- Do you have any fears or dread about your Co-partner?
- Does your Co-partner make you feel different than anyone else?
- Do you feel comfortable with your Co-partner?
- Does your Co-partner appear comfortable with you?
- Does your Co-partner have any personality quirks?
- Do the needs of your Co-partner appear consistent with the needs your relationship's structure fulfils?
- How safe in your relationship do you feel?
- Do you feel that your Co-partner cares about you in your relationship role?

Tactics

- Does your Co-partner hurt you in any way?
- Has your Co-partner ever lied to you?
- Have you ever seen your Co-partner lie to any one else?
- Do you trust your Co-partner to perform his/her role competently and fairly?
- Does your Co-partner trust you to perform your role competently and fairly??
- Are you winning in every way in your relationship?
- Are you happy in every way with your relationship?
- Are you losing in any way in your relationship?
- Are you sad in any way about your relationship?
- Are you starting to worry about your relationship?
- Are you giving up on your relationship?
- Do you feel like you might be the problem on your side of the seesaw?
- Do you feel like it's your Co-partners problem on his/her side of the seesaw?
- What do your friends say about your Co-partner on the seesaw?
- Have your friends ever pointed out any Tactics of yours as being positive or negative?
- Have your friends ever pointed out any Tactics of your Co-partner as being positive or negative?
- Is your Co-partner different in any way from other Copartners you have experienced?